Especially for

Mary Anne Steele,

Keep your brushes going!

Joe Miller
"Cheap Joe"

Untitled by David Miller - Acrylic on canvas - 18" x 24"

Untitled 2 by David Miller - Acrylic on canvas board - 12" x 16"

This book is dedicated
to the memory of my son,
David Tuckwiller Miller.
A fine artist.
1968-2008

OLD WATERCOLORISTS NEVER DIE — THEY JUST WET THEIR SHEETS

OLD WATERCOLORISTS NEVER DIE — THEY JUST WET THEIR SHEETS

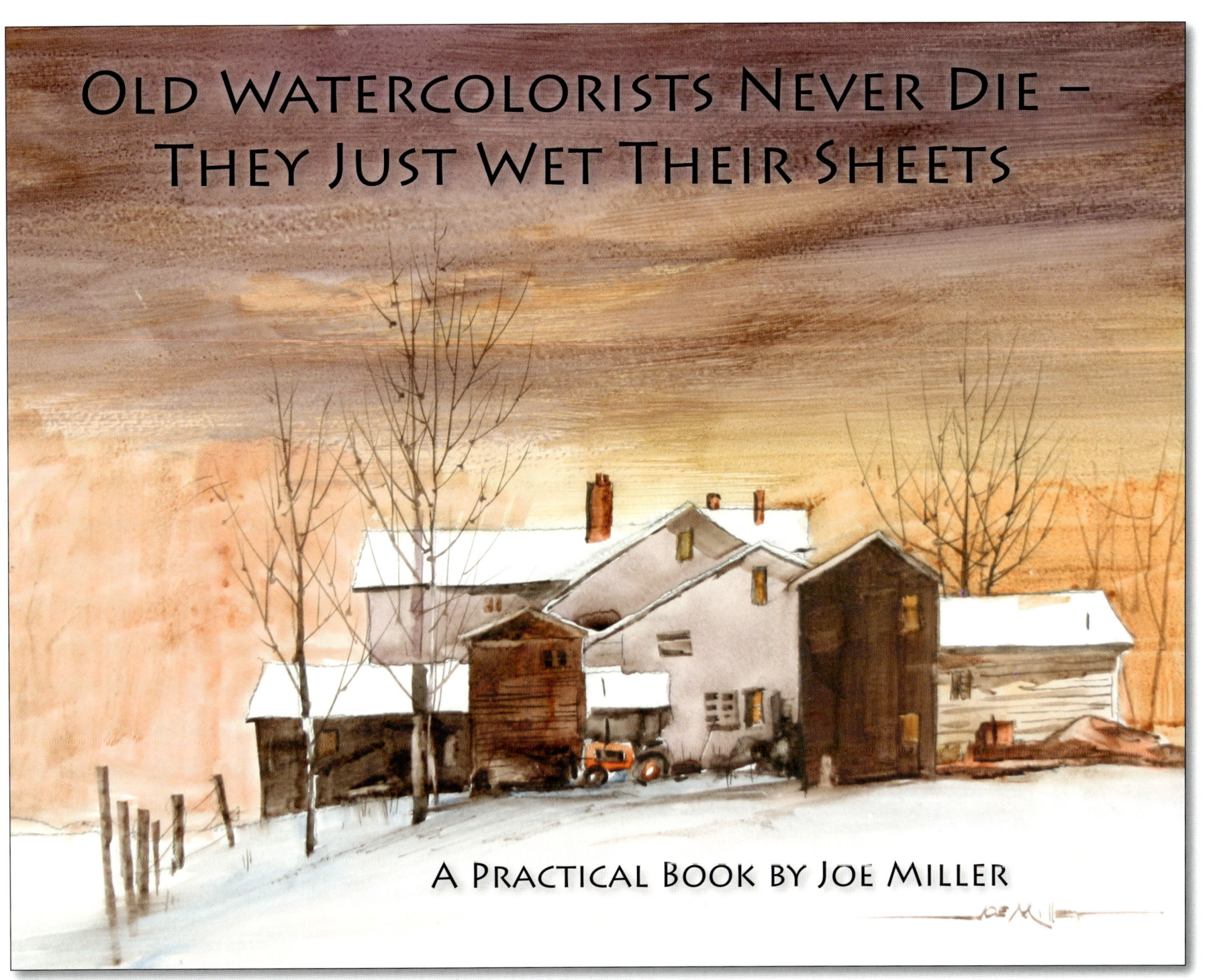

Published by JCM Enterprises
374 Industrial Park Drive
Boone, North Carolina 28607

© 2009 by Joe Miller
All Rights Reserved
Library of Congress Control Number: 2010921538
ISBN 1-890052-10-8

Printed in Malaysia

Cover painting by Joe Miller - *On Hodges Gap Road* • Watercolor on gessoed board • 9" x 12"

Design by Joe Miller and Terry Henry
Layout by Terry Henry

Contents

Preface viii

Chapter 1 – Beginnings in Art—Mine and Yours 1

Chapter 2 – Start by Making Your Mark 12

Chapter 3 – Value 30

Chapter 4 – Pages from My Journals 69

Chapter 5 – Workshop Notes 99

Chapter 6 – Some Seemingly Insignificant Little Things 116

Chapter 7 – Greeting Cards 140

Chapter 8 – Other Stuff 146

OLD WATERCOLORISTS NEVER DIE — THEY JUST WET THEIR SHEETS

Preface

I am honored to have the opportunity to share with you some of my art and, in particular, watercolor. I don't really know why watercolor became my major medium except that before watercolor, (back) when I would see paintings on the wall, it was the watercolors that I most admired and felt I could do. It may be the spontaneity of watercolor that I was drawn to. Perhaps I liked the fact that watercolor is such a quick medium. Or that it's fairly easy to get out, paint, and clean up. For whatever reason, I'm so glad I've had this journey in art. I have met artists around the world, rubbing elbows with artists whose works are in museums and with artists who've just picked up their first brush. Meeting other artists and wannabe artists has been one of the most rewarding aspects of my art venture. I've loved watching people who said, "I can't draw a straight line" or "I have absolutely no talent" take up art, often in their 60s, 70s, or 80s, and crank out beautiful pieces of art that make them feel good and that their family will fight over one day. I tell people it's not about talent so much as desire, want to and have to. Of course there are and have been many people born with talent—Leonardo, Michelangelo, Andrew Wyeth, Jamie Wyeth, etc., but the vast majority of us have about the same amount of talent. I've seen a few people who I honestly thought had absolutely no talent yet who very pleasantly surprised me by excelling in art within a short time. There's an old proverb: give me a person with talent and I'll show you a Painting; give me a person with passion and talent, and I'll show you a masterpiece. So don't let the fact that you think you don't have talent keep you from pursuing art. If it's really something you want to do, then believe me, you can do it. You only have to begin.

Please Read: This book is full of my sketches and value studies. You are welcome to copy from them and use them in other ways for your own inspiration and enjoyment. Do lots of paintings from them, and send me a photo of your efforts. I'd enjoy seeing them!

Old Watercolorists Never Die — They Just Wet Their Sheets

Chapter 1

Beginnings In Art – Mine And Yours

I Wasn't Born

I really enjoy fishing. My favorite is dry fly fishing for trout. I grew up tying flies, building fly rods, and making lead sinkers. I took a correspondence course on taxidermy when I was eleven. So, you see, I've always done artsy or crafty things. I was 45 or so when I began to really see watercolors. I'd looked at paintings done in watercolor, but for the first time I was really seeing the freedom, the brilliance, the look of joy in it. They looked so easy. I can do this, I told myself. I purchased a little set of 8 colors and a brush with a plastic handle of the kind that came in a tin box. I also purchased a watercolor paper pad. All from our 5 & dime store. You can imagine the results. Not too good! I was a pharmacist with Boone Drug Company at the time. That year (around 1984-85) a very good friend of mine, Dr. Rogers Whitener, an English professor at Appalachian State University, gave me three lessons with an art professor at ASU named Noyes Capehart. Some of you may know that name. Noyes is a wonderful artist. I met with him, and he looked at my paintings. He told me that next time I came I should bring my materials so he could see what I was painting with, and he gave me an additional list of materials and told me to go get them.

That list included a Series 7 size 14 pure Kolinsky sable brush (which they don't make anymore because of the rarity of the hair), about 12 tubes of Winsor Newton professional watercolor, 25 sheets of 300lb Arches paper, a John Pike palette, and two or three other little things. The next day I was so excited to go down to Farmer's Hardware, which advertised "If we don't have it, you don't need it." I went there, and they didn't have it! So, I went back to Noyes and told him, "They don't have it, so I must not need it," and he said, "Go get it. If you are going to paint, you need good materials." So, I drove to Charlotte and went to an art store and proceeded to buy the materials to the tune of over $700 – the brush alone was around $350. Would you believe I bought that thing, as cheap as I am? Driving back up the mountain to Boone, I thought, I've lost my mind! What have I done?!

Then, I thought, well, why not sell art supplies in the drugstore—after all, drugstores sell everything. That way, I would have the art supplies I wanted, and I could sell them to other artists, too. So, I began to look for a source for wholesale art supplies, but I really didn't find one quickly. Soon after, I attended the North Carolina Watercolor Society meeting in Durham, and there was a gentleman handing out little tubes of paint. Little tubes of watercolor. I told him, "I would like to talk to you about selling your watercolors." He said, "Okay. Where do you want to sell them?" I said, "In Boone, NC." He said, "Where?

An Artist

Are you going to open an art store?" I said, "No, I'm going to sell them in my drugstore." "Drug store," he said. "You can't sell art materials in a drugstore." I said, "Well, sure I can. We sell everything else. I'm in the middle of downtown Boone, close to ASU, and I'll do really well with it." He said, "Then, I just can't do it." I said, "Why?" He said, "Well, first, you're not going to do any good with it. Second, I sell it to a dentist up in New Jersey, and he doesn't do any good either." I said, "Well, why are you surpirsed? Nobody likes going to the dentist, but everyone likes coming to my drugstore! I'm going to do well." But he said, "No. I just can't do it."

Well, that night, I attended the banquet. At the cash bar, he ordered a margarita. Well, being from the mountains of North Carolina I honestly did not know about margaritas. I knew about moonshine but not margaritas. He drank it rather quickly, and I said, "Would you like another margarita?" "Yes, I wouldn't mind another," he said. So, I got him another one, and pretty soon he drank that one, and I said, "Would you like another margarita?" He said, "Yes, wouldn't mind another." So, I got him another, and after the third one I could tell he was just about two sheets to the wind. I said, "I wish you would reconsider selling me some art materials to put in my drugstore." He said, "Sure, I'd be glad to sell you art materials. I sell them to a dentist up north, who sells the hell out of them. You're gonna do really, really well. I just know you are." I held him to that and the next day made him place the order. That original order came into the drugstore and I think it was $2500.00. It scared me to death when it came. I thought, What in the world am I going to do with all this?

So, I tell people I stuck it between the Exlax and the aspirin, where it did better than either one of those did, so I made a little handmade sign and hung it from the ceiling. To let people know I discounted the materials, the sign read "Cheap Joe's Art Stuff," and it had an arrow pointing down to the few little items on those shelves there. It really didn't do well at all, but I had the list of members from the North Carolina Watercolor Society, and so I simply did a little mailing to them. I hand printed a little sales flyer, ran off 150 copies on the copier, hand addressed each one, and put a stamp on them and mailed them out. And then, believe it or not, those sales did pretty well. So, I thought to myself, I'm onto something here. The first thing you know, we were filling five or six orders a day out of that old drugstore. If you were one of my early customers, I thank you, because what started out in 1986 ended up with today's 50 or so employees and shipping all over the world. So, I thank you for the role you played in that.

Good Advice for a Beginner

When I first took up watercolor many years ago, my friend who was helping me, told me to go buy 25 sheets of Arches 300# cold pressed paper. That's a pack or, in the paper industry, what's also called a quire. "Now don't go buy just a sheet or two," he cautioned, "or you will be afraid of ruining it. If you have lots of sheets, the fear won't be there."

Good advice from Noyes Capehart, retired art professor at Appalachian State University, author, and professional artist. Thanks for helping me on my art journey.

Works by Noyes Capehart

Blue Hydrangea - Acrylic on wood - 2008 - 11" x 22" - Collection of the Artist

The Vicar's Dilemma - Acrylic on Masonite - 2008 - 14" x 17 1/2" - Collection of the Artist

This little oil painting (10" x 14") on some kind of heavy paper is one of my first attempts at art.

Oil on paper - Painted by 12-year-old Joe Miller

I loved fishing and hunting as a boy. I dreamed of one day living in a log cabin, raising all my vegetables, and fishing and hunting for the meat. I guess this cabin represents those dreams. It's fun to look back at what our earlier painting attempts look like. Sometimes it seems I've made a big leap, and other times it feels like I'm still painting like that twelve-year-old. Well, I really wouldn't mind going back to twelve one more time.

This is one of my first watercolor attempts. Notice the little bitty houses in the lower right-hand corner. This must be the land of tiny people! I'm not sure where this place is, but it was painted in January 1983. I hope I've made at least a little headway with watercolor since then. Even my signature has changed. When I was a young boy, a very talented calligrapher taught me to sign my name like this:

Later he taught me this way *[signature]* then *Joe* then, *Joe*, *Joe*

and now I use *[Joe Miller signature]*.

So, yes, I have changed and hope to change more in the years to come.

OLD WATERCOLORISTS NEVER DIE — THEY JUST WET THEIR SHEETS

Be a Bird!

One of my favorite old proverbs: If only the birds that sing best sing, the forest would be silent.

Therefore, if only the artist who paints best paints, the world would be a dull place!

I hear people say, "I don't have talent." Don't buy into that! We all have about the same amount of talent. If you want to be creating art, painting, writing, or learning to play a musical instrument, believe me when I tell you...**YOU CAN!**

Glens of Grandfather - Watercolor - 20" x 15"

A TRUE STORY (AT LAST!)

No one has to like what I do. Sometimes I don't like it...
BUT...
It does make me like my art more when someone else likes it.

A TRUE STORY

At my very first art show I hung a little painting of a landscape with a lake. It wasn't my favorite painting, and I priced it rather low. It was the first painting to sell. I was very pleased until my friend and mentor, Noyes Capehart, came to me and said that it was really a fine piece. I said, "You mean that?" in disbelief. "Yes, it's one of your stronger paintings in the show."

My heart sank to my feet. Even though I'd received the amount I'd asked for, I somehow felt cheated—not by the person who'd bought it but cheated because I hadn't recognized the strength of that painting.

LESSON: When you are selling your first pieces, maybe it would be a good idea to have another artist look at your work. We all need a mentor.

God does not deduct
from our lives
the time we spend
making art!

(or fishing)

Fulfilling Your Purpose in Life

When you do what you love and love what you do, you experience the feeling of true worth and...

9" x 12" watercolor on hot pressed paper. Water-soluble graphite pencil used for background.

... magnetically attract people, places, things, ideas and events that help you fulfill your purpose in life.

– Henry David Thoreau

...and Living in the Present

We fulfill our purpose when we live in the present moment. I find myself regretting things in my past or worrying about what the future holds and therefore not living in the present moment. I find that making art forces me to be with myself at that moment. It's a little like meditation. I can get lost in my art. I think that's living in the present.

East Tennessee Homestead - Watercolor - 22" x 30" - Private Collection

Chapter 2

Start By Making Your Mark

If you've never painted, then you have to start somewhere. I suggest doodling or making marks. You won't need to invest much, just a pencil or pen and paper. It's been said that the best way to improve your painting skills, is to improve your drawing skills. So just start drawing or doodling whatever is in front of you. It gets to be more and more fun the more you do it.

Doodling and Staying Loose

For some people, doodling is like grits in the South: they is automatic. I ordered breakfast in Georgia once and asked the waitress if grits came with what I ordered. She responded, "Mister, grits is automatic!"

So to me and lots of you, doodling while doing something else is automatic. I've read that people who doodle while listening during a boring talk or while talking on the phone actually improve their retention. Plus, who knows—you might end up with some doodles that are the basis for a painting.

I like making marks. I get as excited as a five-year-old on Christmas morning when I discover a new pen, pencil, crayon, etc.

I make marks—or as some call it, doodle—while I'm on the phone or watching TV. Sometimes I fill in the value—thinking dark and light. It's fun, but it also helps with value and drawing.

Some of my favorite pens to sketch with: Pitt, Sharpie, Copic, and Fredrick Graff "Twigger-Rigger" from my woods.

Doodlings

Pen drawings with pencil value added.

A VERY LOOSE PAINTING

I hear it all the time — "I want to loosen up." I think what we're saying is I want to paint with more freedom. I want to color outside the lines. By holding this pen at the top gives a looser line. Is that a real word? Looser. So, if I hold my paint brush at the tip I bet my paintings will be "looser".

The writing on this page was done with a black, medium point Faber-Castell Pitt Artist Pen and waterproof, lightfast, India ink.

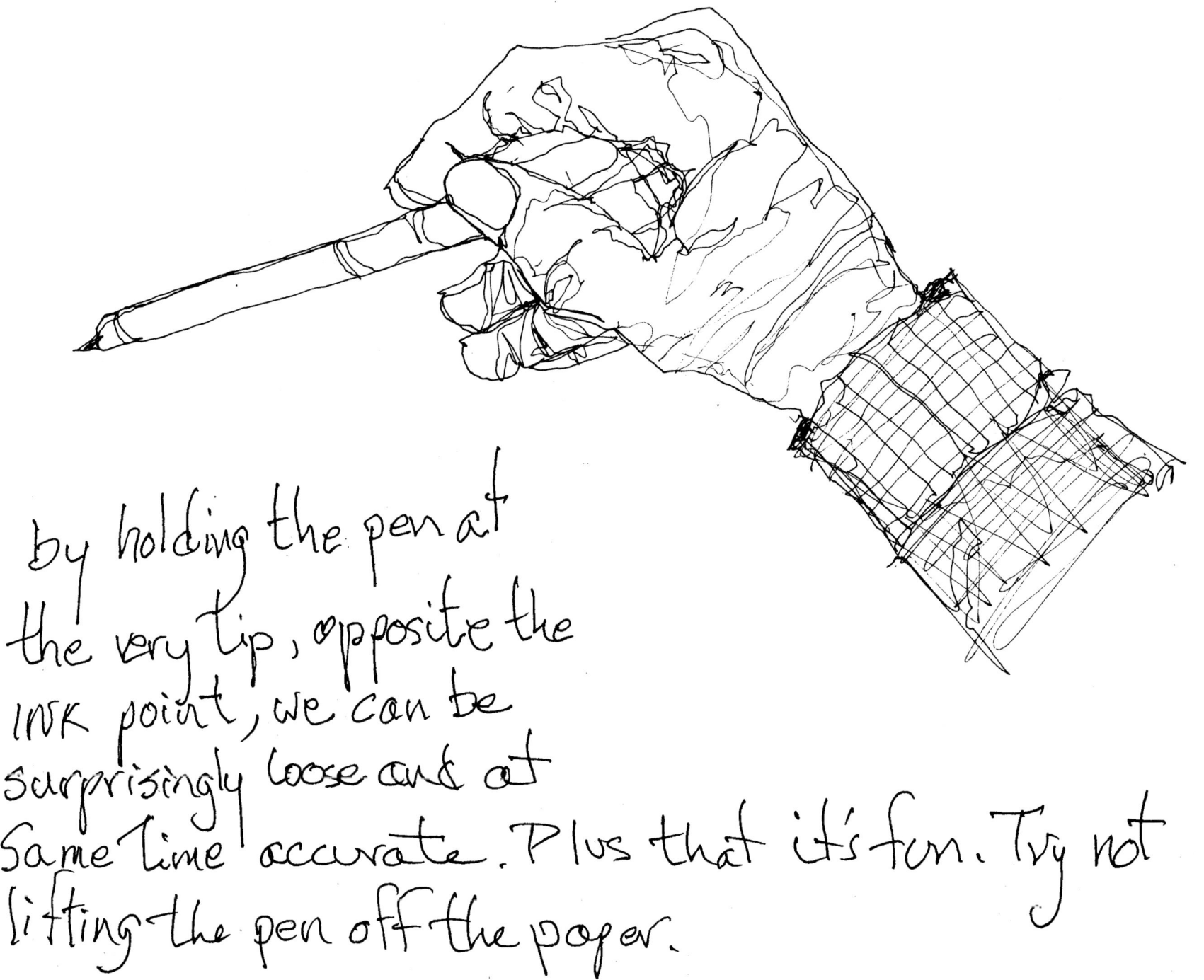

by holding the pen at the very tip, opposite the INK point, we can be surprisingly loose and at same time accurate. Plus that it's fun. Try not lifting the pen off the paper.

Looseness! Or Loose Marks

A few members of my family, drawn with a fine Pitt pen held at the end for looseness! Is that a real word? Try holding your pen or pencil by the end with thumb and two fingers to draw anything. Don't lift the pen up from the paper if you can help it. This is called contour drawing, and it's really fun.

Looseness! Continued...

This was all done with a fine (F) black Pitt pen by Faber-Castell. Waterproof and permanent these are great pens! I've fished all my life, and I've never caught a fish that looked like these.

Looseness! Continued...

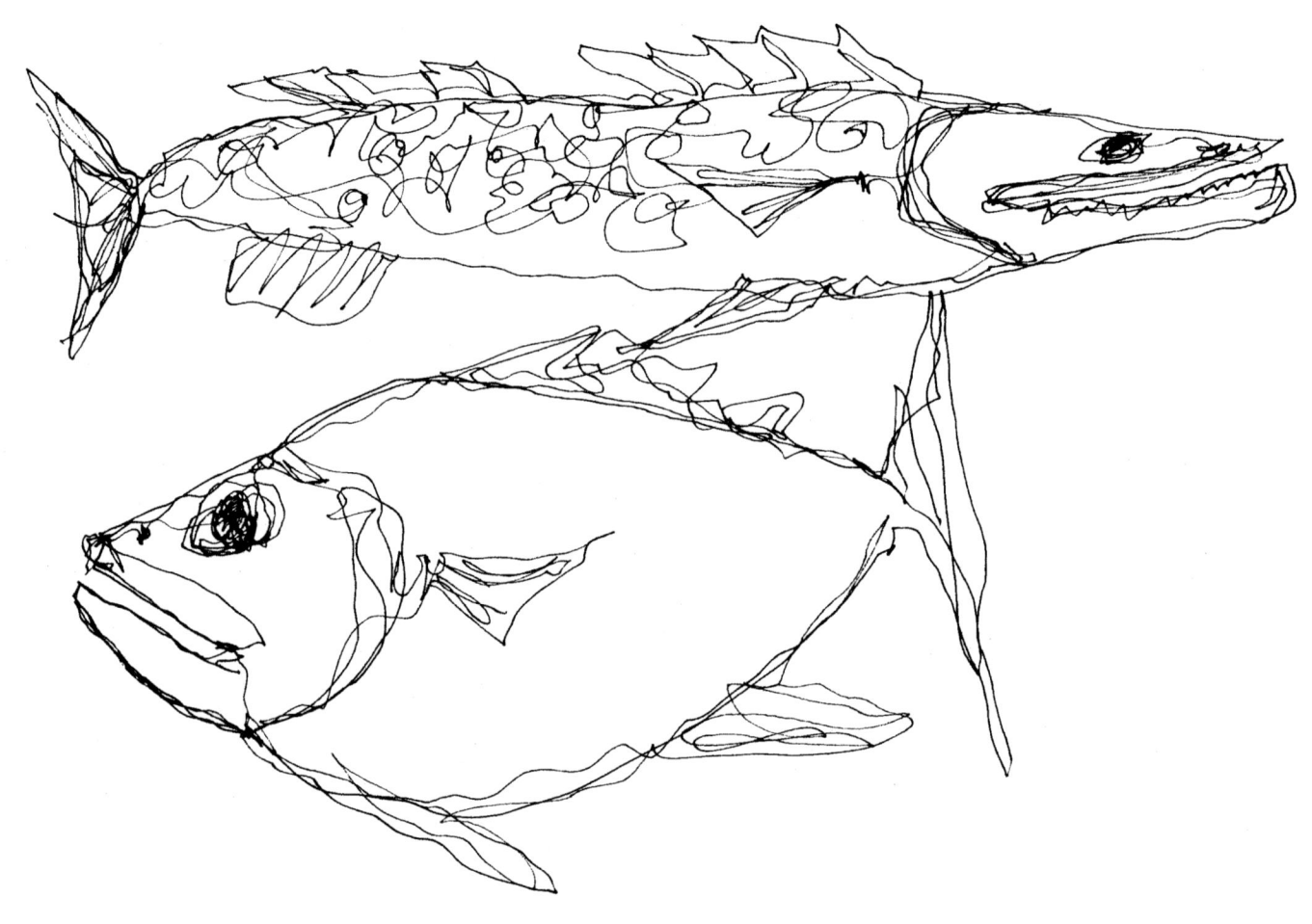

These wild-looking fish were drawn with a size 0.1 Copic black pen held at the very end of the handle by thumb and two fingers. It's a great way to stay loose.

The Graff "Twigger-Rigger"

Fredrick Graff discovered this tool that makes the most incredible marks and is FREE at the Twigger-Rigger store. And, wait, if you order by midnight they will double your order-absolutely free! Well here's how to get your new free revolutionary art tool.

Take a little walk in the woods and pick up several twigs. You may sharpen one end with a pocket knife or leave them "au natural."

Here's the first one Fred gave me. I have it hanging on my studio wall, and like Fredrick Graff, it inspires me to make my own marks and be creative.

1. Use ink. I like Sumi or India.
2. For different value, try diluting ink with H_2O.
3. Dip Twigger-Rigger in it.
4. Hold at opposite end and make marks.
5. Fun? You bet!
6. Good marks? The Best!

A loose painting – lots of splatter, dabbing, wet in wet – just having fun.

Watercolor on Watercolor on Watercolor - 20" x 30"

You *will* get discouraged. You *will* have times when you want to give up. Read the following until you have it memorized. This is the S-Curve of Creative Learning, and every creative person I know understands it. This "S", although sideways, shows us how a creative or artistic person experiences the highs and lows of making art. We begin our journey at day 1 and move up the S-curve almost effortlessly day by day–until one day, WHAM! We feel as though we're on a roller-coaster downhill. This is where most people give up. **BUT**, if you continue your struggle, you'll find yourself going uphill again, and you will soon reach a new plateau. Remember though, if you stick with your art, you will experience this up and down throughout your career. Leonardo, Vincent, Pablo, and every other artist who sticks with his trade will go through this. Yes, you will despair, but "this too shall pass" and you will be on your upward journey soon. The nice thing is that you never go below the last valley, and you always rise above the last plateau. Don't give up!

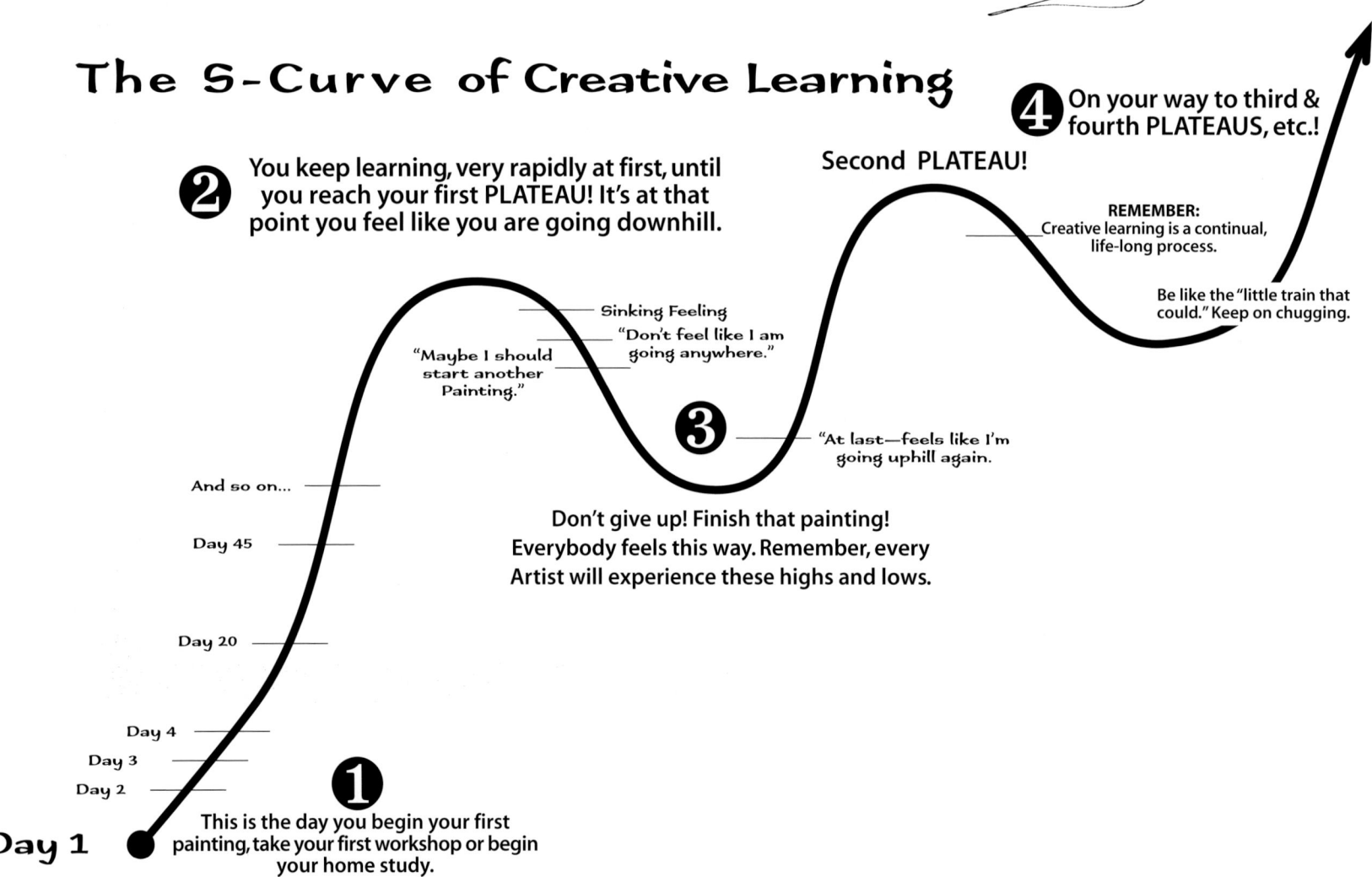

OLD WATERCOLORISTS NEVER DIE — THEY JUST WET THEIR SHEETS

The Little Voice in My Head

Isn't it funny how we listen to that little voice inside our heads. I hear it loudest when it says, "Joe, that's the worst painting I've ever seen." But when it brags on me, I can hardly hear it at all. I'd like to know what gives that little voice the right to critique my work? When and how did he become the expert?

From now on, when he starts his "You are no good" stuff, I'm going to bong him on the head and tell him, "GO AWAY!"

A page from a journal done in 1997 that even today evokes good memories.

Gotta Be A Fish Here Somewhere - Watercolor - 22" x 30"

Smile. Yep, smile and act like you know what you're doing. When you finish a painting, smile, stick your chest out, and say, "I did that!" At my age, I have to like some of what I do. I don't have all that long to perfect this thing called art, so I'll just pretend. I'll secretly pretend that at least one little area of my painting is perfect and hope the viewers will see that area!

START BY MAKING YOUR MARK

Laugh, Laugh a Lot!

Did you hear the one about sister Gertrude on her dying bed?

Seems as though all the sisters knew sister Gertrude was on her last hours, so they gathered around her bed and asked, "Is there anything you would like before you depart this world for the next?" She thought a minute and said, "A glass of warm milk would be nice.

The sisters went to the kitchen to fetch her milk but could find none. One of the sisters discovered a bottle of Scotch in a cabinet and told the others that perhaps in her condition, sister Gertrude wouldn't know the difference. So they warmed a glass and took it to her. She drank it, and again the sisters asked if there was anything else she would like. "Yes, another glass of the nice warm milk would be nice." They brought her another glass of warm Scotch, which she drank.

One of the sisters asked, "Sister Gertrude, are there any words of wisdom or advice you would give us before you depart?"

"Yes," she said, "Whatever you do, don't sell that cow!"

After my mother died, my brothers and I were going through some of her stuff and found this little clipping she had probably cut out of "Reader's Digest" or some other publication.

Dear Stockholder:

Our records indicate that you own stock in American Can, National Water and Universal Gas. Our advice to you is to sit tight on your American Can, let your water go and pass on the gas.

Sincerely,
Dr. I.P. Freely, President
P.S. Kleenex tissues touched a new bottom today.

Chapter 3

Value
(not in dollars)
Dark & Light

This section contains drawings, value studies, and doodlings I've scratched out. Feel free to use any of them as a beginning for your paintings or drawings.

3B Pencil

American Journey Lucky Penny

Black Sumi Ink

20 40 80
French Grey Prismacolor

Values – The Dark and Light Sides!

Pen and Ink

Value is dark and light. Every color has value, some much more than others. But value doesn't necessarily have color—it can be just black, white, and shades of grey.

Pen and Ink and pencil

Values (darks and lights) are seen best when facing the sun, especially if you squint. Try it, then face the other way with the sun to your back and I think you'll see what I mean.

Pen and Ink

Some more sketches done on location...so much fun!

Pen and Ink and pencil

VALUE 31

Here are six pencil drawings of the same house shape, each with a different light source.

When doing value studies on location, it helps to see the value better if you squint. By squinting we take the color out and leave value (dark - light). Another easy way is to use a piece of red or blue acetate. Hold it up while looking at the subject—this also takes the color out, and you will be able to see the darks and lights better.

Value studies, pen and ink drawings—value added with a 2B drawing pencil.

HOWARDS CREEK IN WINTER.

BAMBOO

VALUE

A page from my journal where I sketched with a water-soluble 8B graphic pencil and then ran a damp brush over the sky. These pencils are really fun and great for value studies.

Value Paintings Are Easy If...

you choose only one color to do an entire painting.

In this little sketch I used only Quinacridone Gold.

Colors with strong value, like the darker colors, work best—
dark browns, dark blues, dark violets, etc.

Landscapes are what brought me to art. I would see a painting of a landscape or village scene and think, I can do that. I still really enjoy going to a new area and finding new scenes to paint. I get really turned on just doing a value study of my new scene. I don't always do a value study, but I get better results in my paintings when I do the value study first.

My Valleys in Winter - Watercolor - 14" x 30"

My Fields - Watercolor - 15" x 20"

VALUE

Sketched on location at Huntington Beach State Park, S.C., using black fine-point Pitt pen.

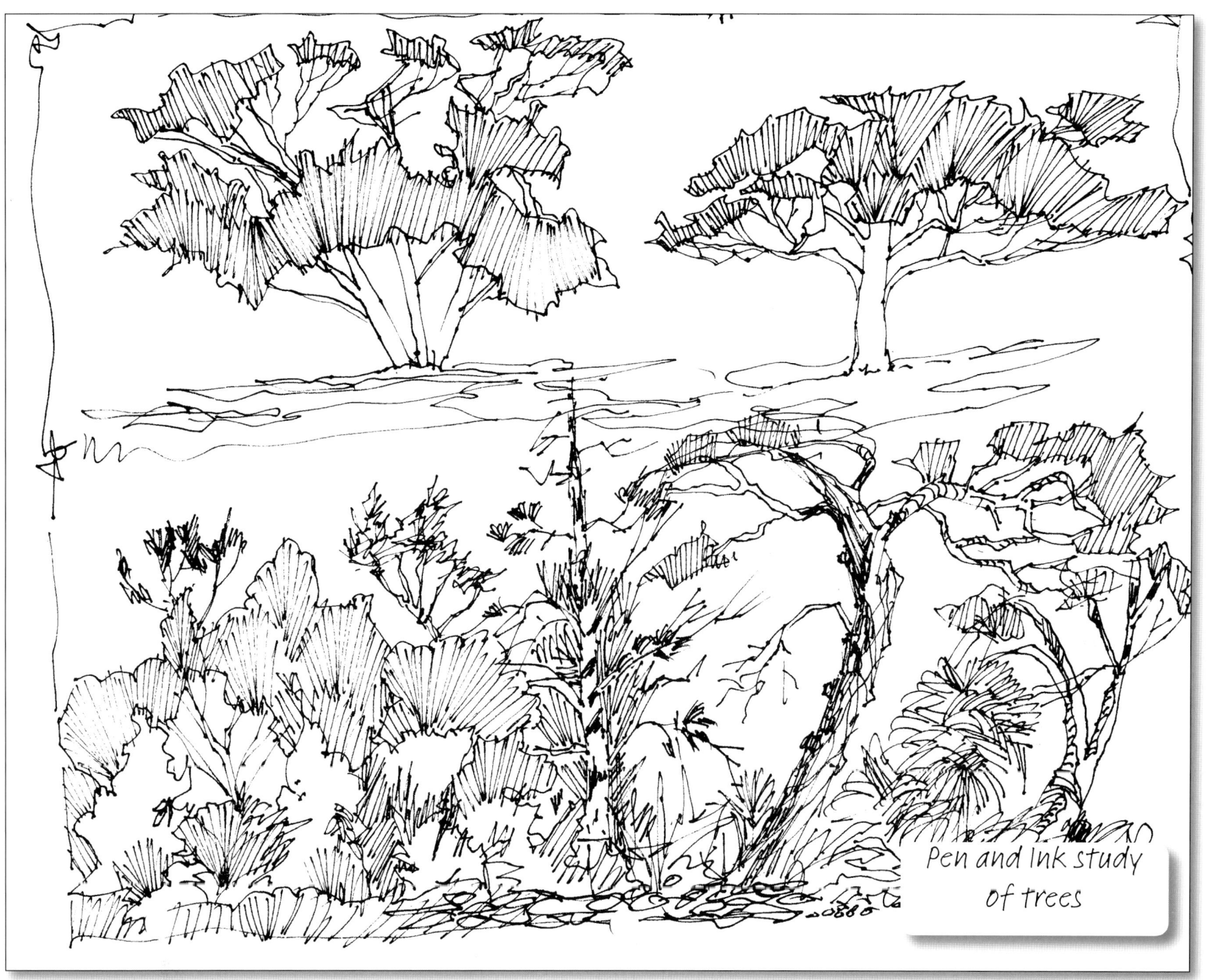

Pen and Ink study of trees

VALUE

An old homestead near Mama Lee's. Mama Lee was my grandmother who lived in Todd, N.C.

Mama Lee's Neighbor - Pen and Ink, pencil

I have several three-ring binders filled with sketches I've done on loose sheets of paper or torn out of a notebook. I look back and see just how simple some are, and in others I see more. When I flip through these notebooks, I'm instantly taken back to the place and time I did them—unlike taking photos, where I look through them and wonder where I was and why I took them.

Glen's Place

VALUE

Value study of <u>Downtown Boone</u>, drawn with a black, ultra-fine Sharpie pen.

Downtown Boone - Watercolor - 22" x 30"

2-minute sketches done in Gerald Brommer's class

VALUE

Value study of Cone Mansion Carriage House

Pencil sketch done somewhere on coast of Maine - 2005

I usually note the location, date, etc. on my sketches. If I don't, like with this one, I will forget exactly where I was.

MANCHESTER, VT 11/20/02

Journal Page

Why are artists so alive? I think it's because they continue to learn, grow, and remain enthusiastic about what they do.

VALUE 51

Oct 11, 2008 — Stopped to have the car washed. I looked around and here were these wonderful old trucks and a "dozer". I don't believe any would start, much less run but they did make a great "family photo".

From my journal — pen and ink on hot pressed paper

If you've ever had the good fortune of visiting Boone, North Carolina, and the Mast General Store in Valle Crucis, you'll understand this quick sketch of the the old building that houses the Mast Store. The walls and floors really are crooked and lopsided. But the owners, John and Faye Cooper, and the employees are straight as an arrow. It's a wonderful place to visit, plus buy some clothes, shoes, and candy. I can spend hours in and around the Mast Store sketching and painting.

A sign on my door from John Cooper reads: "When so many artists have turned to drugs, It's refreshing to see a druggist turn to art. Your friend John Cooper."

Sketched on location in Port Clyde, ME, with a black Sharpie on 140# hot pressed paper (American Journey Journal).

Sharpie Permanent Marker. Brown and black ultra fine point.

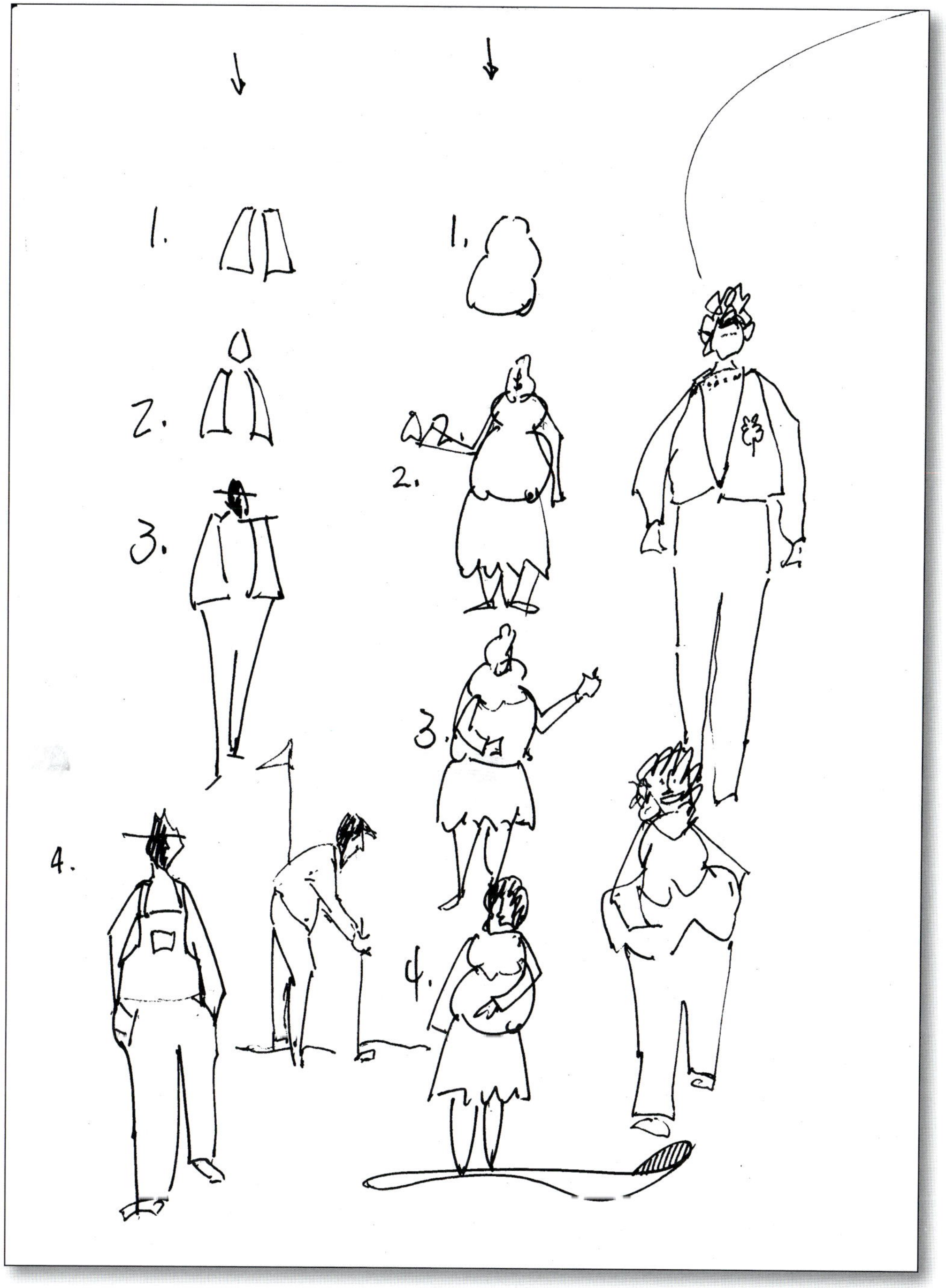

VALUE

Laugh

Laugh at yourself. Laugh when you goof up. Laugh when you put the wrong color in the wrong place.

Laugh when you forget what it was you wanted to do. Laugh again when you finally remember!

Laughter is a good thing. It's much better to laugh than to cry!

The old home at Elk Creek Mountain that Aunt Hazel lived in. 10/29/06

My First Watercolor Lesson!

One of the first books I read on watercolor was <u>My Way with Watercolor</u>, by Ted Kautzsky. In the first lesson he allowed one color, which was Alizarin Crimson. This is all about value. Look what mood I created with just one color.

In Lesson 2 we could use two colors—Alizarin Crimson and French Ultramarine Blue.

VALUE

In lesson 3 we used Alizarin Crimson, French Ultramarine Blue, and Yellow Ochre.
When he got around to five or six colors, Ted Kautzsky said, "We are rich." I highly recommend the book
<u>My Way with Watercolor</u>!

Frank Francese, of Colorado, is a very fine artist and teacher. Here are two value studies and the paintings done from them by Frank. Frank's value drawings are works of art by themselves. They are done with markers like Prismacolor or Copic. You may see more of Frank's work at:

www.ffrancese.com

Value

Value study for _Frosty Feeding_

In one of the early workshops I attended, I roomed with a fellow named Charles Sharpe. Charles was a very fine artist even then. I admired his work but was really taken by his value studies. They were great! Charles showed me how he did them and gave me helpful tips on keeping sketches and value studies for reference.

Frosty Feeding by Charles Sharpe - Watercolor - 22" x 30"

Here's one of my value studies for the painting that was used on the cover of our local High Country Magazine.

Just How Important Is the Light?

There was a man and his wife who lived way out in the hills past Boone, toward Tennessee. She was heavy with child, and late one day she told him that he'd better go fetch the doctor. The baby was on its way. So, he saddled his horse, rode into town, fetched the doctor, and hurried back home to his pregnant wife. When they got there, the doctor told him to gather some hot water and clean cloths. Then, the doctor asked if he didn't have some better light. The man ran to get a lantern in the barn, and when he returned, the doctor told him to hold it up, because the baby was coming. In a minute, the doctor said, "Congratulations, you have a fine baby boy." "Oh, this is good!" the new father exclaimed. "I'll go down to the pub and have a beer with the fellows to celebrate my new baby son." "Not yet," said the doctor, "Hold on, hold the light up. I believe there's another one coming. Oh, look, it's a big baby girl!" "Oh, this is really good!" the father said. "I'll just go down to the pub and have two beers – one for my boy and one for my girl." "No, hold on and hold the light," said the doctor. "There's another one on the way." The father looked at the doctor and asked, "Doctor, do you think it's the light that's attracting them?"

Chapter 4

Pages from My Journals

These cover several years, and you will see dates on some of them. It's one of my favorite things to do when my wife Lynda and I travel. She drives, I look. Works out great for both of us as she's a good driver—me, well...

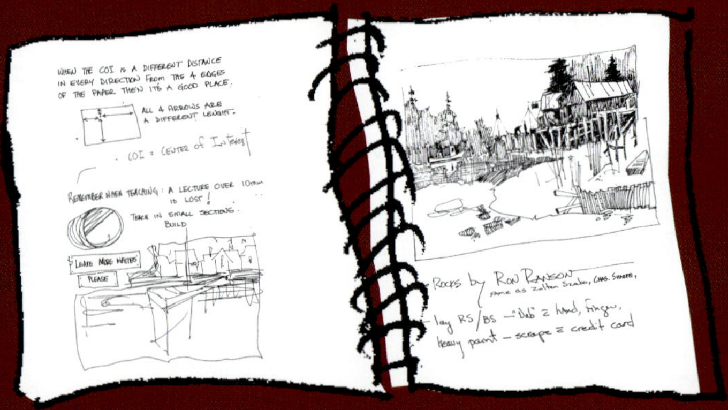

Through my art years I've kept journals. I haven't been as faithful to journaling as I wish I had, even though I have filled a couple dozen. I've seen some journals by my artist friends that knocked my socks off. Don Getz does wonderful ones. Brenda Swensen does fabulous ones and has written a book on journaling, which you can get from Cheap Joe's.

Journaling

 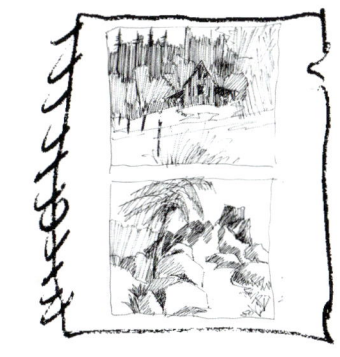

I usually do my journaling on location. It's hundreds of times better than a photo. When you journal on location you never forget where you were, what you felt, or who came up to you. I start out by taping around where I am going to do my painting. Next, I draw with a pencil or waterproof pen, then paint. After the painting dries, I remove the tape—this gives a nice, neat, clean edge for my journal, which I like. Often, I will do a larger painting from these little journal paintings, but I never seem to get the spontaneous look that my journal has.

  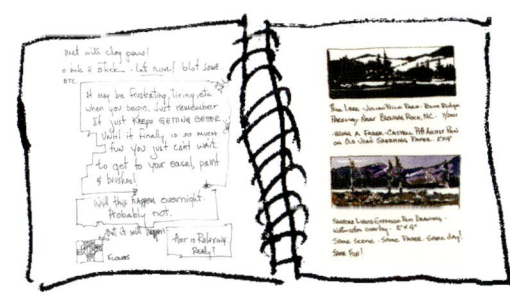 

PAGES FROM MY JOURNALS

Here's How I Begin...

I use artist tape to create a nice clean border when I'm journaling and occasionally on my watercolors. Good tapes come with more than enough stick-it-to-em. So BEFORE you put the tape on your paper, put it on your jeans or shirt, pull it off and then put it on the watercolor paper. This may save you heartache, as it will prevent the tape from tearing your watercolor paper. Be sure to allow your painting to dry completely before removing the tape.

Step 1: After you've put the tape on your shirt or jeans, place it on the journal page where your painting will be. I like the 1-inch artist tape.

Step 2: Draw with pencil or pen. If pen, be sure it says "waterproof" on the barrel or it might smear. Notice in the upper right-hand corner, my little sun on the top to remind me where the light is coming from.

Step 3: Add color. Notice the paint on the tape. Don't be concerned about paint on the tape, as you will of course remove it when finished.

Step 4: Add pen and ink if you'd like.

See the messy tape. Now watch what happens when we remove it.

PAGES FROM MY JOURNALS

Step 5: Carefully remove tape. Now add interesting comments. This is the way the actual page looks in a journal. With a ruler, run a line around it for another mat. Add a light value with a Prismacolor marker grey 20% for shadows.

This is the entry in my journal for May 21, 2007 — Drove to New River in Alleghany County today to fish for small mouth and anything else that would bite. Took the wrong road and came around the bend to find this old farmstead. Looked inviting, so I did this little sketch. The owner, Mr. Greenshoes (acutally they were Hooker's Green Shoes) came to check me out. We had a nice talk about art, farming, fishing, and life. (Great day! And a new friend). Had a cheeseburger, fries, and Coke at Mary's Diner. Umm good!

Page from a journal done in Maine

78 OLD WATERCOLORISTS NEVER DIE — THEY JUST WET THEIR SHEETS

Old Watercolorists Never Die — They Just Wet Their Sheets

Street scene done in Beaufort, NC

Old Watercolorists Never Die — They Just Wet Their Sheets

New River at Greenway Covered Bridge.

OLD WATERCOLORISTS NEVER DIE — THEY JUST WET THEIR SHEETS

The Springmaid Pier at Springmaid Beach in Myrtle Beach, South Carolina, has always been a favorite subject for the artists who go there to study.

> The border around this page from one of my journals was done with a brown Prismacolor pen using a ruler for straight edge. It's a little like framing it.

shadows on mt. are constantly changing but always show the contour of the mt.

FOUND GOODIES

WHILE LYNDA STAYED AT THE CABIN AND READ I TOOK A WALK ALONG THE BEACH AND FOUND...

A PIECE OF SHINGLE LIKE OUR COTTAGE IS COVERED WITH

Painted on a piece of shingle found on the Pemaquid Beach and glued in my journal

Plastic lobster trap tag found on Pemaquid beach and glued in my journal

A TAG I THINK IS FROM A LOBSTER TRAP. IT IDENTIFIES THE OWNER.

WHAT TREASURES AWAIT ME NEXT STROLL?

ANOTHER I.D. TAG FROM A LOBSTER TRAP?

I ALSO FOUND TWO LOBSTER TRAPS, THE METAL WIRE KIND, A BUNCH OF ROPE, A NICE LOB TRAP BUOY THAT I COULDN'T QUITE REACH BECAUSE OF SEAWEED. THE SEAWEED IS SO THICK AND SO SLICK THAT I WASN'T ABLE TO WALK ON IT. KEEP SLIPPING. MAYBE IT WILL WASH CLOSER TO SHORE AND I'LL GO FETCH IT.

PAGES FROM MY JOURNALS

Practice Makes Perfect

Well, not really. There's no perfect in art. We always think we can improve on what we've just done.

We go to an art class and watch the instructor do a demo. Effortlessly. We have it in our heads, so we go back to our table to do the same thing—and fail miserably. We try and fail again. Then a light comes on like a bolt of lightning, and suddenly we have it or at least some of it. Why? Because we have to experience it time and again. A musician doesn't hear his teacher play a tune, then immediately go repeat it.

Musicians practice, gymnasts practice, players of football, baseball, and every other sport practice. Yet for some reason we artists think we can go for months without painting, then pick up a brush and be right where we were. Doesn't work that way for me. It takes me a while to get back in the groove.

Sinking Feeling

Todd's Store 10-15-07
Rode my bike up Big Hill Road — so pretty along New River. One of those "I'd like to can today" days!

When I was just a boy, almost every Sunday my family climbed in our old car and went to visit my grandparents in the little farming community of Todd, North Carolina. I loved going there. When we went for lunch, that was really special because we had chicken and dumplings and lots of different vegetables. And of course, pies, cakes, and usually sugar cookies for dessert. And real milk—milked by hand from a real cow and kept cool in the spring run at the back of the kitchen. After lunch, we would all find our way to the front porch where the "old people"—my uncles, aunts, and grandparents— would tell stories and relate events from their childhoods or the previous week. I remember my grandmother, whom we called Mama Lee (her real name was Leander), would sometimes begin by saying, "I had this sinking feeling…" Being so young, I didn't really understand what that meant. I do now! It's that feeling you get when you're painting and suddenly something goes wrong. Oh no, wrong color, too big, too little, etc. I bet if you've painted long, you know exactly what Mama Lee meant when she said, "I had this sinking feeling…" I think that a blank canvas or blank piece of paper can cause a sinking feeling. We put the first few colors down, and there's another sinking feeling. It seems each step can and may bring on this feeling. We overcome this by completing the painting. It's like climbing a mountain, step by step. Finally reaching the top, we can see the whole mountain. Each step in picture making erases the sinking feeling. Don't let the negative voices in your head win! Keep on keeping on.

A page from one of my journals

View from Rm 331 - Equinox Hotel · 11/16/02 · Awoke to a beautiful, quite snowfall. Arrived here - Manchester, Vt. 5:00 PM 11/15 - nap, met Barbara, Gary & Cathleen for dinner. Barbara is teaching workshops, Gary is gen. mgr. of Equinox & Cathleen is editor of Amer. Artist Mag. —

On a little dirt road about 5 miles N. of Manchester, Vt. 11/16/02 – Meet with Barbara and Cathleen to learn about the workshops she will be teaching here. Had lunch and Lynda & I drove out in the country side to sketch – so very beautiful, about 3" of clean new snow. The landscape here is very "Wyethesk". Love it!

Journal page

Wed. April

I see a seagull pick up a shell, probably a clam, fly in a circle up several feet and drop it. The bird did this repeatedly each time checking to see if she could get the morsel out for dinner. There's no one here but me and the birds in this big expanse of beach. I watch gulls, loons, ducks and shore birds. I found a lobster buoy that broke away during a storm and best of all, in every direction, a painting!

A lone lobster man circles into "my cove". He drops a trap and moves a ways then drops another. I think season is just begining.

Journal page

Journal sketch
6" x 10"

Except for the red accents, this little sketch was done entirely with Sumi ink by diluting it with water to obtain the lighter values. A "Twigger-Rigger" made the trees.

More "Twigger-Rigger" playing

Watercolor and ink - 6" x 10"

Dilute the ink with water for a lighter value. Add watercolor to the ink for an intensifying effect – like reddish black.

Manchester, VT. 11/20/02

Watercolor over water soluble 8B graphite pencil

Pages From My Journals

A journal page

Pages From My Journals

Molding Our Own Lives

Artists, writers, sculptors, musicians, and other creative people are very fortunate to be able to create beautiful works that we all can appreciate and enjoy, but the most valuable work we can create is a happy, useful, productive life. I have been one of those fortunate individuals (I often call it luck, but in my older years believe it's much more than that) who have been somewhat able to mold my life. I think we all mold our own lives—we just are not aware of it. I come more and more to believe it's attitude.

I, like all other humans, have had a share of discomfort, distress, heartaches, and worries. It's not a matter of whether there will be problems or not, but rather of when they will come. So, ultimately it boils down to how we perceive these problems, how we handle them and whether or not we handle them well or allow them to overcome us. Life can be good, but we have a great responsibility to make sure it is!

Making art is simply a matter of momentum... at some point you simply must do it!

Chapter 5

Workshop Notes

I've had the opportunity to take quite a few workshops, and I always take copious notes. I am constantly referring back to these pages—especially if I'm in a slump and need a "jump start." The following are pictures of actual pages taken from my notebooks.

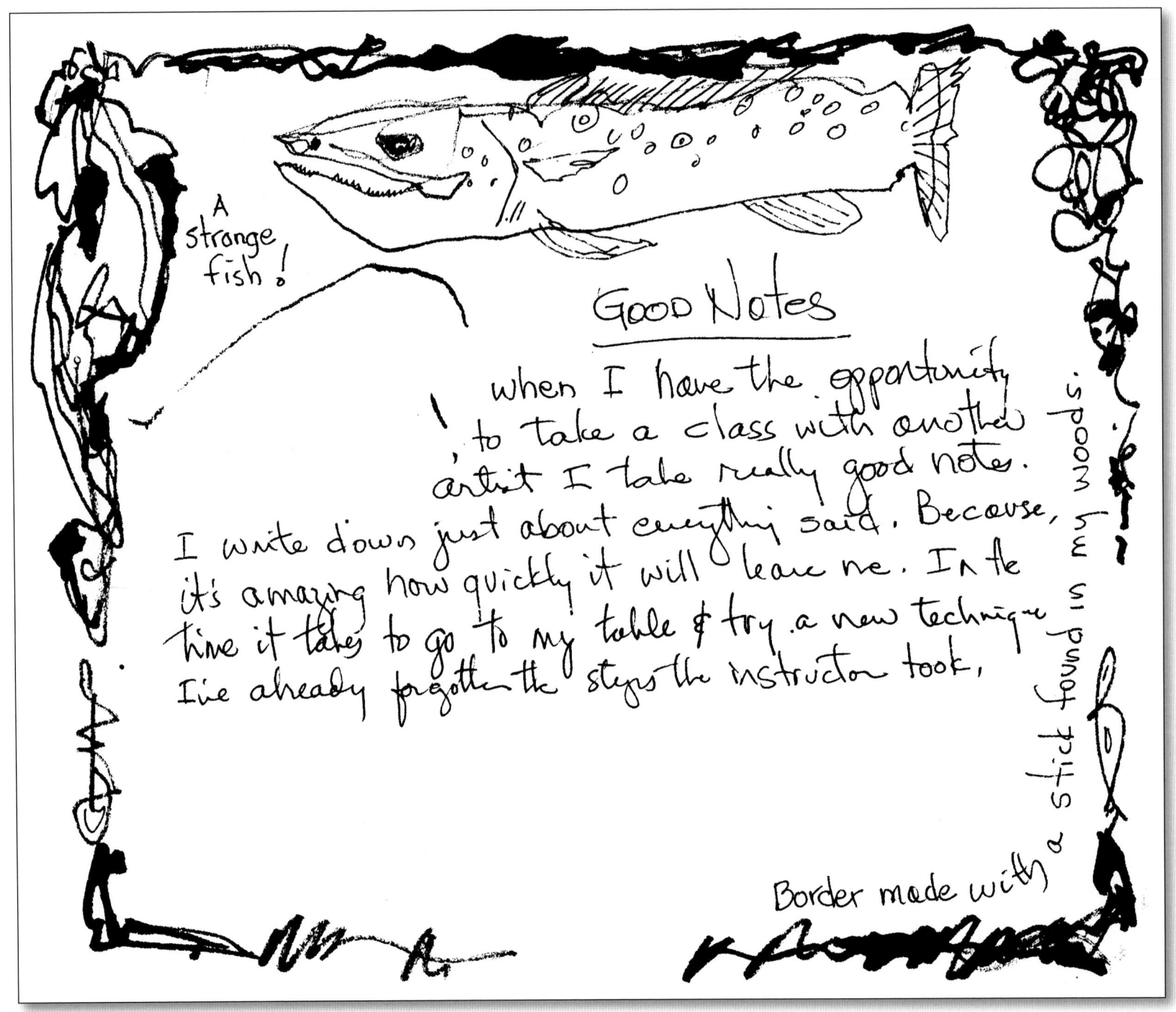

A strange fish!

Good Notes

When I have the opportunity to take a class with another artist I take really good notes. I write down just about everything said. Because, it's amazing how quickly it will leave me. In the time it takes to go to my table & try a new technique I've already forgotten the steps the instructor took.

Border made with a stick found in my woods.

River Scene
From Photograph

Fall Colors

FUM	RS	Quin Gold
		AC
CY		BU

1. Draw on WC paper.

Start from background with painting.

AC + FUM for bckgrd. on wet area – very delicate. Trees onto this w/w – in very distant. Light colors on 1st – Yellow. (very nice = mauve)

Keep building value.
Rigger work while still damp.

Do DETAIL on DRY PAPER

When painting from a photo, do a value study and see how much you can leave out and still capture the essence of what you want to say.

Now, hide the photo and use your value study for your painting. It will have "YOU" in it. If you paint from photo it may have more of photo and little of you.

I was worried that you would have difficulty reading my printing.

Hope it's no problem
WELCOME

Don't be afraid of the dark...
It's the base in your painting!

Hold rigger at the very tip of handle – will keep you from being tight. — any brush for that matter!

When the COI is a different distance in every direction from the 4 edges of the paper then it's a good place.

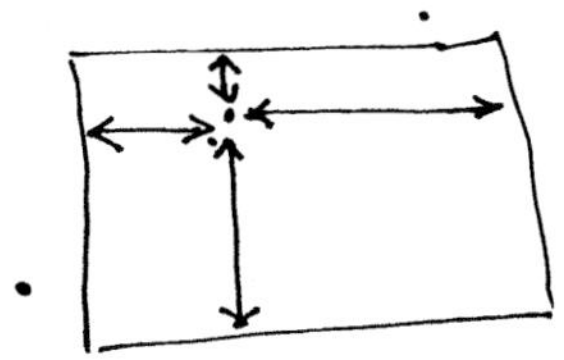

All 4 arrows are a different lenght.

COI = Center of Interest

Remember when teaching: A lecture over 10min is lost!

Teach in small sections.
Build

LEAVE MORE WHITES
PLEASE

WORKSHOP NOTES

Workshops Should Be Called Funshops

My friends Larry and Helen O'Connor have taken over 60 art workshops in the past 8 or so years. They attended ten alone in 2008. I could name lots more artists who have taken many workshops. I can name professional artists who regularly attend workshops. If you ask them why, you might be surprised at their answers.

"It keeps us young."
"It's entertaining us while we learn."
"It's the only time I really work at art."
"I wanted to jump start my art—and it did."

I have the opportunity to attend many workshops at our Cheap Joe's studio. I love going in the workshop and watching the demos and hearing the instructor talk about his or her approach to art. I've attended many workshops and learned something new in each and every one. I take extensive notes so I can refer back to them.

Pages from Workshops

* Take one of Serge's — change people, colors, etc. & it's yours.

Demo 3/19/03

Group of people in NYC in rain.

— pencil marks for location of feet, heads.

All done in dark color. (Bl./vio./Grey) Vary.

— Keep all wet & at end, scrape in rain ≡ screw driver like tool.

— Lastly, put in bldgs - Light wash, grey / Brown / grey. Vary.

Send Serge

I've had the privilege to be with Serge Hollerbach a few times.

This page from my notes taken in 2003 still has meaning for me and recalls a great workshop by Serge.

Serge Holerbach class
Springmaid Beach
Nov '05

Some artists paint what they see and what's there, while others paint what should be there.

Serge modeling for the class.

The way to the room of fame and fortune is long and narrow, and the waiting room is full! Some will enter through a door marked Pull, and some through a door marked Push.

It's great fun to be learning a new hobby, regardless of what that hobby is. I used to believe that you should have an understanding and at least some knowledge of art before pursuing it. Now I know you can take up art and enjoy it to the utmost and gain knowledge of art as you travel this journey. You need not know anything other than that it's something you really want to do.

So, what are you waiting for? Go for it!

Always make your colors darker and brighter than you want because in watercolor they always dry lighter.

When I attend a workshop, I take lots and lots of notes. Some of the things I note would not make sense to others but do to me. Here are a few pages from workshops with Gerald Brommer and Ron Ranson.

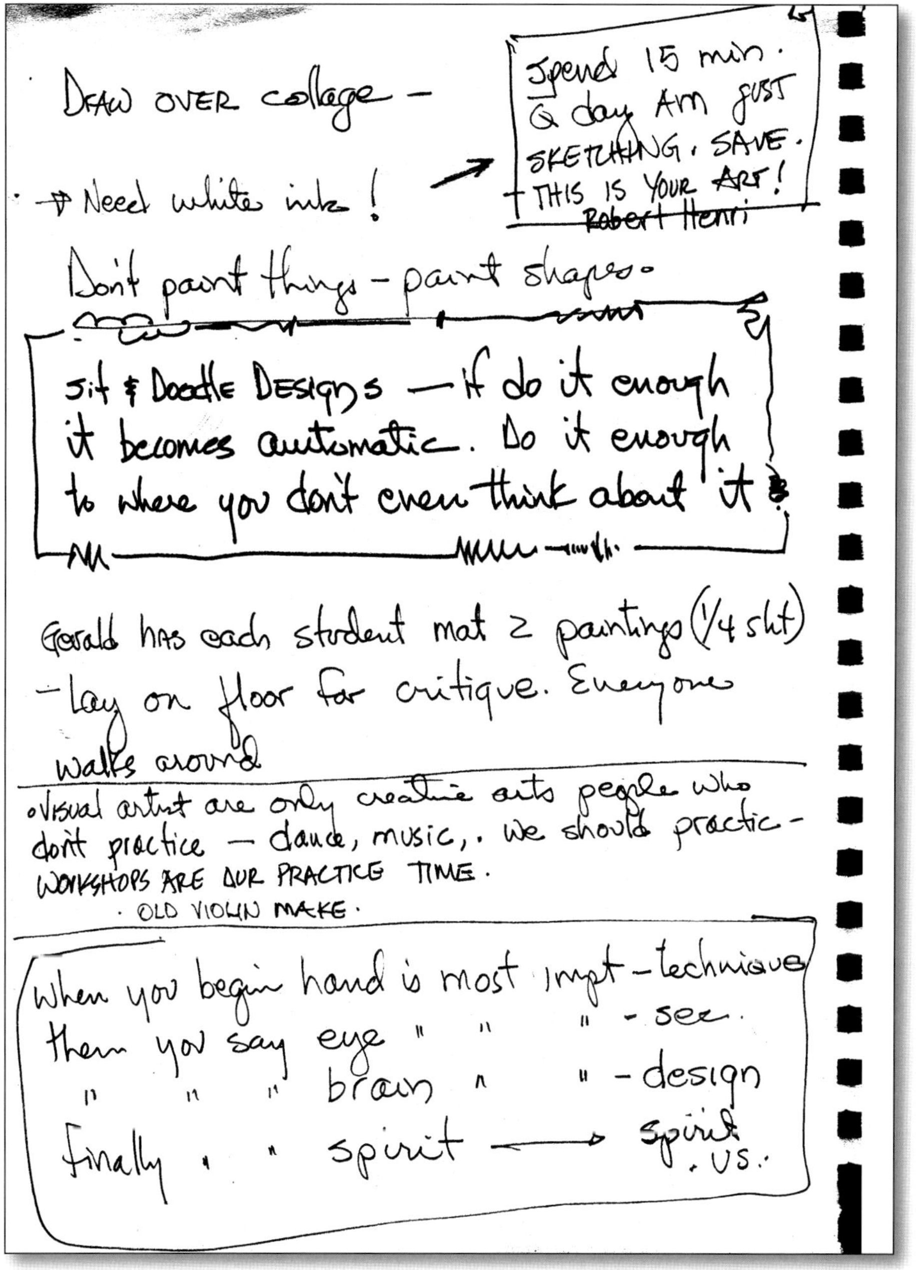

(sketch 1: village street scene — labeled "Corners QUITE please!" and "QUITE please")

(sketch 2: hillside houses — labeled "QUITE please!" and "QUITE please")

(sketch 3: cluster of houses and trees)

DRAW OVER college —

• Need white ink!

→ Spend 15 min. a day am just SKETCHING. SAVE. THIS IS YOUR ART!
— Robert Henri

Don't paint things — paint shapes.

Sit & Doodle Designs — if do it enough it becomes automatic. Do it enough to where you don't even think about it.

Gerald has each student mat 2 paintings (1/4 sht) — lay on floor for critique. Everyone walks around.

• Visual artists are only creative arts people who don't practice — dance, music,. we should practice — WORKSHOPS ARE OUR PRACTICE TIME.
• OLD VIOLIN MAKE.

When you begin hand is most impt — technique
then you say eye " " " — see.
" " " brain " " — design
finally " " spirit ⟶ spirit
                              vs.

Gerald Brommer · Springmaid · 11/11/07

Line/shape workshop.
Line outlines the shape — usually.
Now, want <u>line to be independent of shape</u>.

Henry Fukahara
96 yrs old

Leave pencil lines — they become part of painting.

Wonderful for doodlers! Like me!
<u>An unfinished look</u>! Let viewer fill in.

TODAY
1. Do at least 4 sketches — line only of subject.

   Quite corners.

2. Do color shapes over. line ⟶ line doesn't follow color!

Line 1st — color over   OR
Color — line

Pages from some more of my workshop journals

"I should get the nobel prize for that!"

- Can add shapes over shapes = color or line.

"The more tools to work with the more fun" Gerry

IF IT GETS TOO DARK — USE white Ink or Gouche.

When putting color over line — you may protect whites of buildings, people, etc.

— Draw over lines to make heavier lines — <u>Variety</u>!

"Make line joyful, have a good time!"
Journal in the painting.

108   Old Watercolorists Never Die — They Just Wet Their Sheets

Weighted line — thin to thick

THIN LINES NEXT TO HEAVY.

TOO MANY OF SAME SIZE LOOKS TOO MUCH LIKE A COLORING BOOK.

← Busy area

← Quiet area

* In focal area put down smaller, darker shapes.
* Use wash of white Gouache, blot, to lighten.
* May change colors in focal areas. repeat lightly somewhere else.

Nov 13, 2007   JERRY BROMMER
Collage.   9:00 AM TALK. DEMO
                9:15 we WORK!

1. Stain = pale colors several pieces of paper.
   Put on paper towel to dry
   9:40 - demo → 5 min!
2. Make @ least 4 studies - simple lines.

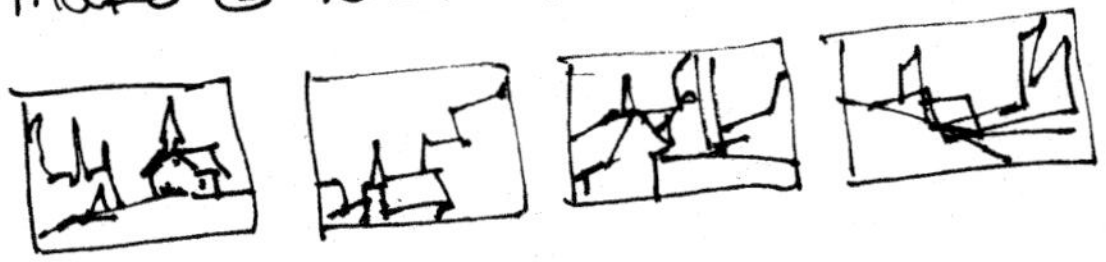

3. Pencil drawing on paper.
   Draw a box for steple or dome as they are usually drawn too big
   ← MUST FIT

4. INK OVER pencil OR collage —
5. Lay paper shapes ———. Draw then paper — VARIETY

WORKSHOP NOTES

↑ CORNERS! ↑ CORNERS!

THINK Corners

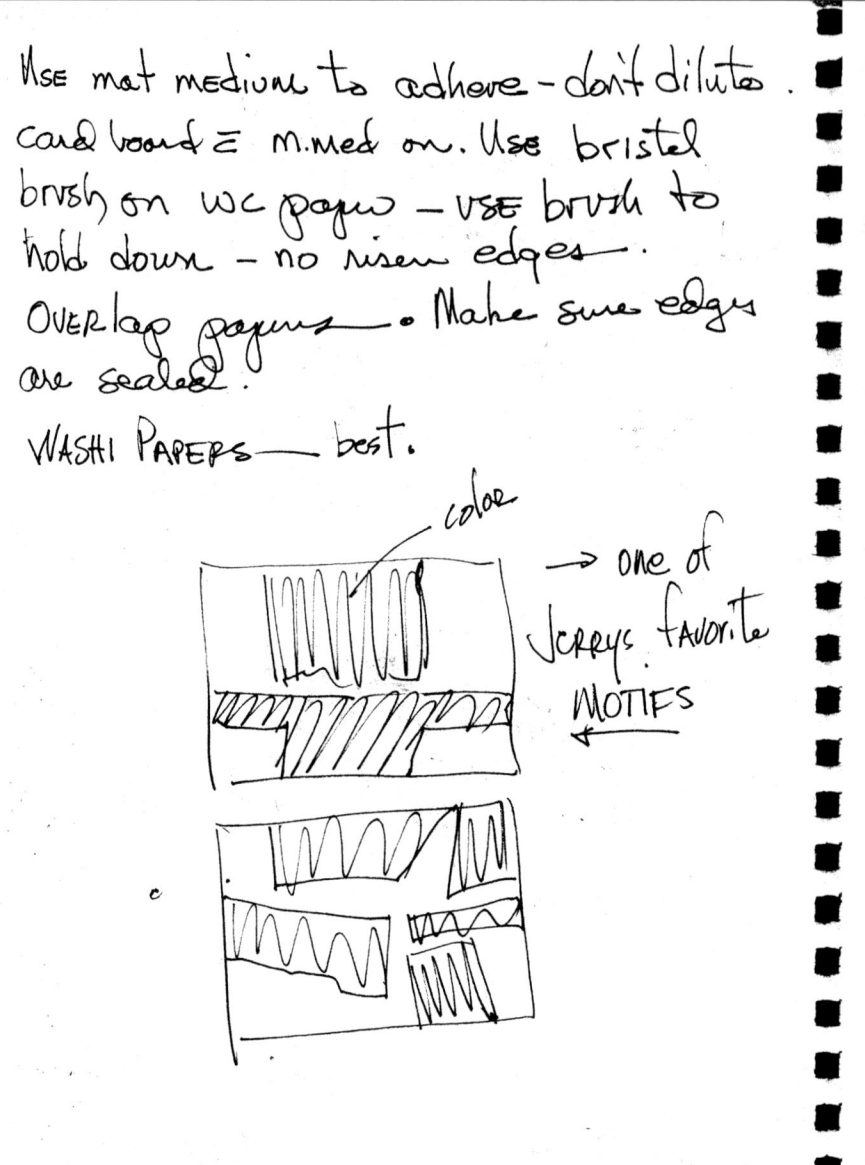

Use mat medium to adhere — don't dilute. Cardboard = m.med on. Use bristle brush on w.c. paper — use brush to hold down — no risen edges. Overlap papers. Make sure edges are sealed.

WASHI PAPERS — best.

← color
→ one of Jerry's favorite MOTIFS

Pages from Ron Ranson workshop

Workshop Notes

wet will clog pens!
o ink = stick. Let run! blot some.
etc.

It may be frustrating, tiring, etc when you begin. Just remember It just KEEPS GETTING BETTER. Until it finally is so much fun you just can't wait to get to your easel, paint & brushes!

Will this happen overnight. Probably not.

But it will happen.

Flowers

ART IS RELAXING. REALLY?

Ron Ranson Again — 11.7.07

"Don't demand more confidence of yourself than you've earned." In other words you can only do what you can do at this time. As you paint more, you will be able to do more.

Ron Ranson may have one of the finest, simplest, quickest way to do skies.

Some of the people who've influenced my life & my art.
1. NOYES
2. CHAS SHARPE
3. SKIP LAWRENCE
4. TONY COUCH
5. JANET WALSH
6. CHENG KHEE CHEE
7. DON ANDREWS
8. FRANK WEBB
9. GERALD BROMMER
10. JAMIE WYETH
11. STEVE DOHERTY
12. TED KAUTZKY
13. Fred Graff
Vincent · Andrew · Jamie

IF IT LOOKS RIGHT WHEN YOU PUT IT DOWN, MAKE IT DARKER! WC ALWAYS, YES ALWAYS DRIES LIGHTER.

You must keep many mats @ your works. It blocks out everything else while you paint. Someone space to put over your painting around the table & allows us to see where we are going. And when it's time to stop.

Back to Ron Ranson
Tues., Nov. 6, 2007

Snow Scene

Foreground
BV, PG, AC

| CYP | AC |
| PG | RS |

Keep same colors as in sky.

Leave lots of open spaces in trees. Someone said "make room for the birds to perch."

12 x 16 wc block

① Wet, watery AC over RS
② W/W AC.
③ PG + AC

When your finished — stop!

Pull PG + AC down lightly — some RS as move down.

Yellow at top to reddish yel or salmon @ horizon.

Connect clouds while wet → looks more realistic.

blossom — pulling wet paint on a 1/2 wet or 1/2 dry (either way) paper. To prevent, simply make sure you've less H₂O on your brush — more color than where you are going on the painting.

A beginning watercolor always scares me. It doesn't look right. Can't quit. Don't let sinking feeling win.

My good friend Fredrick Graff has invented (I'm not so sure he would choose "invented") the all new, revolutionary, Twigger-Rigger! Here it is — Go for a walk and while walking, gather some twigs — dry ones are best. With a pocket knife sharpen one end and make a small slit — like a fountain pen — Here's what you will end up with —

← SLIT

Now dip the "pen-end" in your paint. Hold it at other end with your thumb and two fingers... jerk it over the paper for unusual marks ooo ooooo

I'm Scared

Every time I teach a workshop I get scared! I'm afraid I will run out of things to show, I'm afraid I'll fail at a demo, I'm afraid they won't like what I do—and the list goes on and on. So, I work very hard for days before a Workshop. Perhaps we are the same way every time we begin a new painting. We are scared of the white surface, we are afraid to fail—and some are afraid to succeed! How do we overcome our fear? We don't have to overcome it, we just have to keep on keeping on. Believe me, I know about being discouraged. Thank goodness I know about keeping on, too!

Chapter 6

Some Seemingly Insignificant Little Things

These little tidbits have made a difference for me. Hope you benefit from one or two!

Hot or Cold, Please?

I find that I am usually more pleased with my painting if I decide on the temperature before I begin. Not temperature as in thermometer but with a warm or cool color.

I could flip a coin and pick one. It has nothing to do with the scene, time of year, etc. It really is a personal decision by the artist. A snow scene may be warm and a tropical summer scene may be cool. It all depends on the colors you use.

If I choose warm, I will use warm colors - yellows, oranges, reds, colors seen in a fire—with a little cool, as with blues and violets. If I choose cool, I will use predominately cool colors - colors at the North Pole—with a little warm. I try to think 80:20. If warm - 80% warm color, 20% cool.

Making this decision helps me set a "mood" in my painting.

Warm Colors

  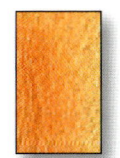  

Bumble Bee Yellow | Raw Sienna | Quin. Gold | Royal Amethyst | Rambling Rose

Cool Colors

Cobalt Blue | French Ultramarine Blue | Joe's Blue

How Does That Color Make You Feel?

Certain colors evoke certain feelings. Red—like Marilyn Monroe lipstick—now that's certainly sexuality, passion, energy, heat, fire.

How about orange? Think restaurant chairs or Wendy's signs. I'm told that orange whets the appetite and reminds up of emotion, feelings, attachment, etc.

Red:	passion, grounding, energy, heat, fire, sexuality
Orange:	emotion, hunger, feelings, attachment, sexuality
Yellow:	heat, self image, fragrance, willpower, sexuality, freshness
Green:	healing, love, compassion, caring, forgiveness, harmony, balance, sexuality
Blue:	calmness, expressiveness, creativity, communication, sexuality
Indigo:	mindfulness, insight, vision, wisdom, sexuality
Violet:	service, knowing, bliss, oneness, sexuality
Black:	void, strength
White:	purity, cleanness, freshness

As of today, this is my studio palette. I use the American Journey Cavalcade palette. I love it. It's porcelain! It's heavy—weighs 5 lbs.—and stays put even with the most vigorous digging for color and mixing. My palette changes fairly often as I discover new colors. That's part of the excitement of art — discovering new colors, new papers, new brushes, etc.

The dark colors, of course, give strong value and lighter colors-lighter value. The lighter values are usually the brighter colors —yellows, oranges— while darks are blues, violets, dark greens, etc.

An easy way to see what value each color has: simply look at your palette and squint. As you look at this page, you will see light colors on the left and dark on the right.

SOME SEEMINGLY INSIGNIFICANT LITTLE THINGS

Don't Be Cheap Like Me

You can use cheap paint and cheap brushes to learn this thing called H_2O color, BUT you cannot use cheap paper. You must use 100% acid free, cotton rag paper. It's more expensive in the beginning but "cheaper" in the long run, as you will learn quicker.

Never, ever throw away watercolor paper just because the painting didn't work.
You Can...
1. Turn it over on the back – paint on it.
2. Scrub it – even put it in the bathtub, soak it for 30 minutes, and then scrub it with a stiff brush.
3. Gesso it – paint on it for an unusual effect. Allow gesso to dry before painting.
4. Cut it into cards or make great bookmarks!

Don't try to fail just so you'll have a failed painting! But if you did try to fail and you did, would you have succeeded or failed? WOW. Now that's deep.

*Keep your first paintings – date 'em, look back.

Ten Little Things that Are a Big Help

1. Begin your painting with BIG brushes and use them until you can't stand it before picking up a smaller one.

2. Don't get picky! Save details until the very end.

3. Arrange your material so you are comfortable with it. If you are right-handed, have water, palette, etc. on your right. Paper in front of you. Left-handed? Water, palette, brushes on left.

4. Buy a tube squeezer. It will pay for itself in no time.

5. Have several mats at your art table. Putting mats around your paintings will let you know better where you are.

6. Fill the wells in your palette. You can't paint with the paint in the tube, and you will waste less by filling the wells. If you squeeze a little watercolor in your wells, it will dry out and be useless.

7. Use transparent watercolor to glaze. Opaque colors tend to "muddy."

8. Paint as if there are no rules. Do whatever it takes to make a better painting. How 'bout using white paint? Go for it! Remember, whatever it takes.

9. Leave more whites on the paper than you think you'd like. You can always cover them up.

10. No one can tell you when you are finished. Only you know that.

No Drips Please!

Arrange your materials so you are comfortable with them. If you are right handed, have water, brushes, etc on your right.

Lefty: materials on your left.

You will have fewer "drips" on your painting.

I'M RIGHT HANDED.

A VERY SHORT TABLE !!

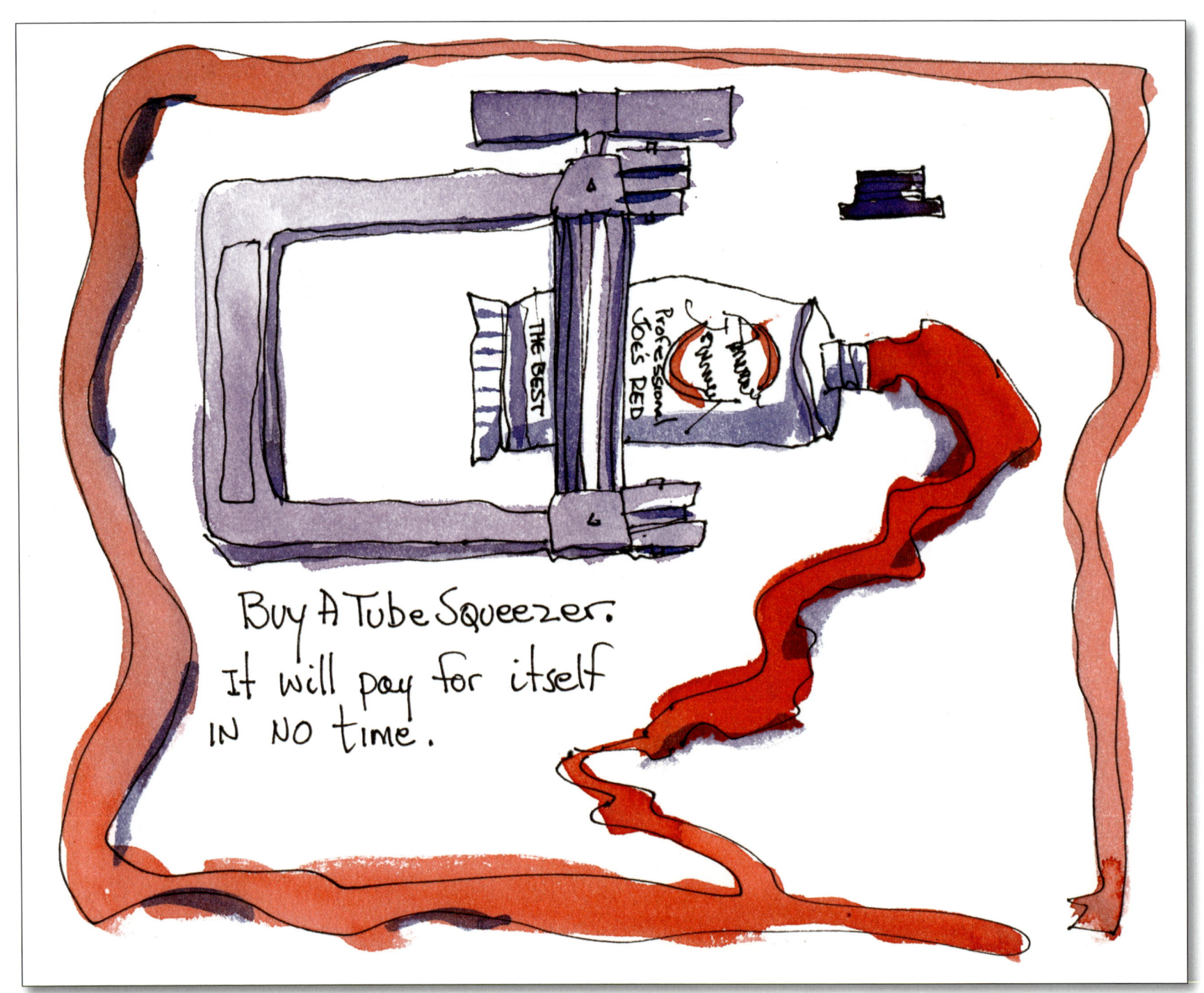

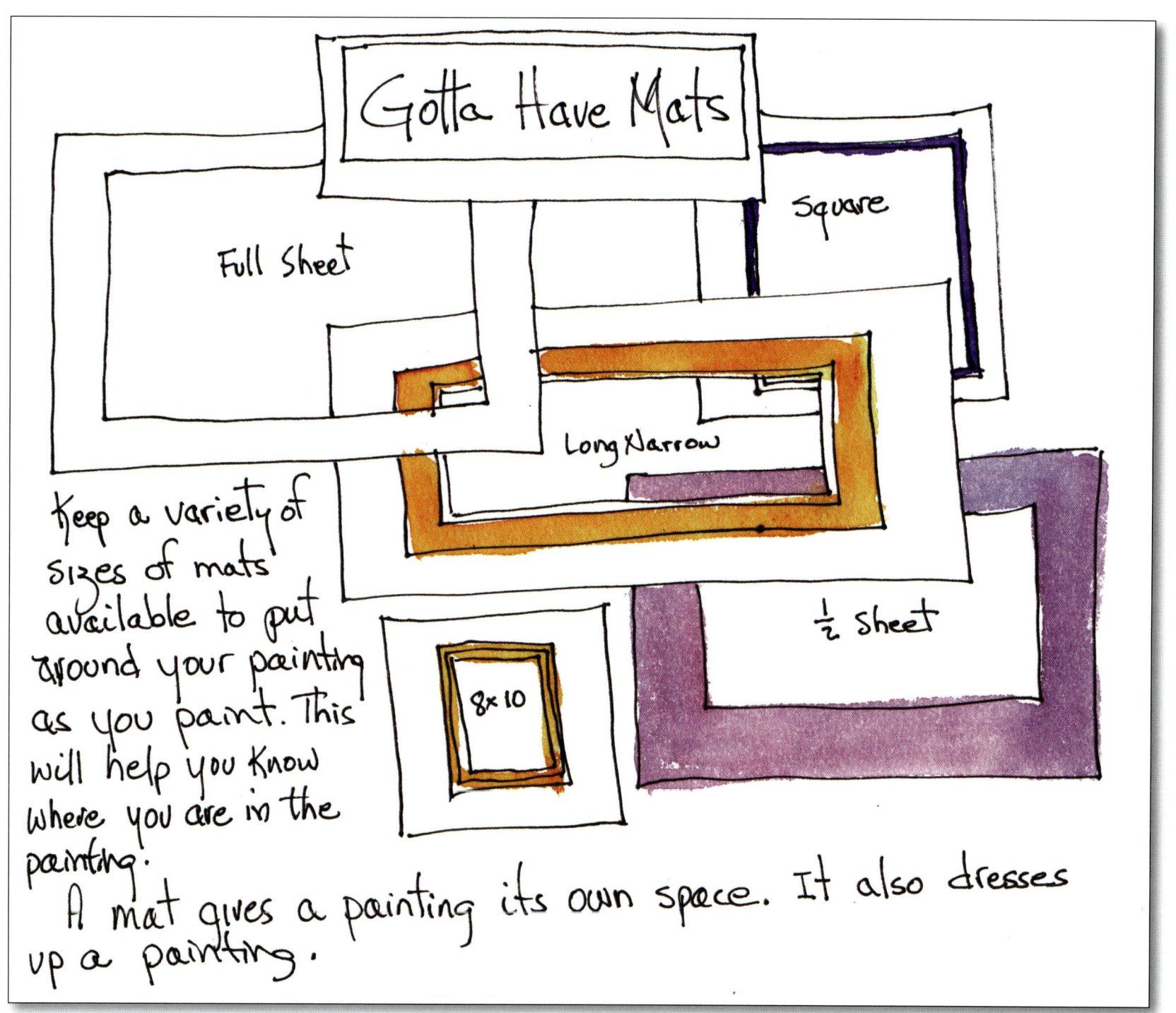

SOME SEEMINGLY INSIGNIFICANT LITTLE THINGS

A Little Dab Won't Do

Fill the paint wells in your palette.
I mean **really** fill them.

You can't paint with the paint in the tube, so squeeze it out and fill your paint wells.

You actually waste less this way.
If you put a "dab" in your well, it will dry up and fall out one day!

Be brave and go for the Gold — fill those wells!

SOME SEEMINGLY INSIGNIFICANT LITTLE THINGS

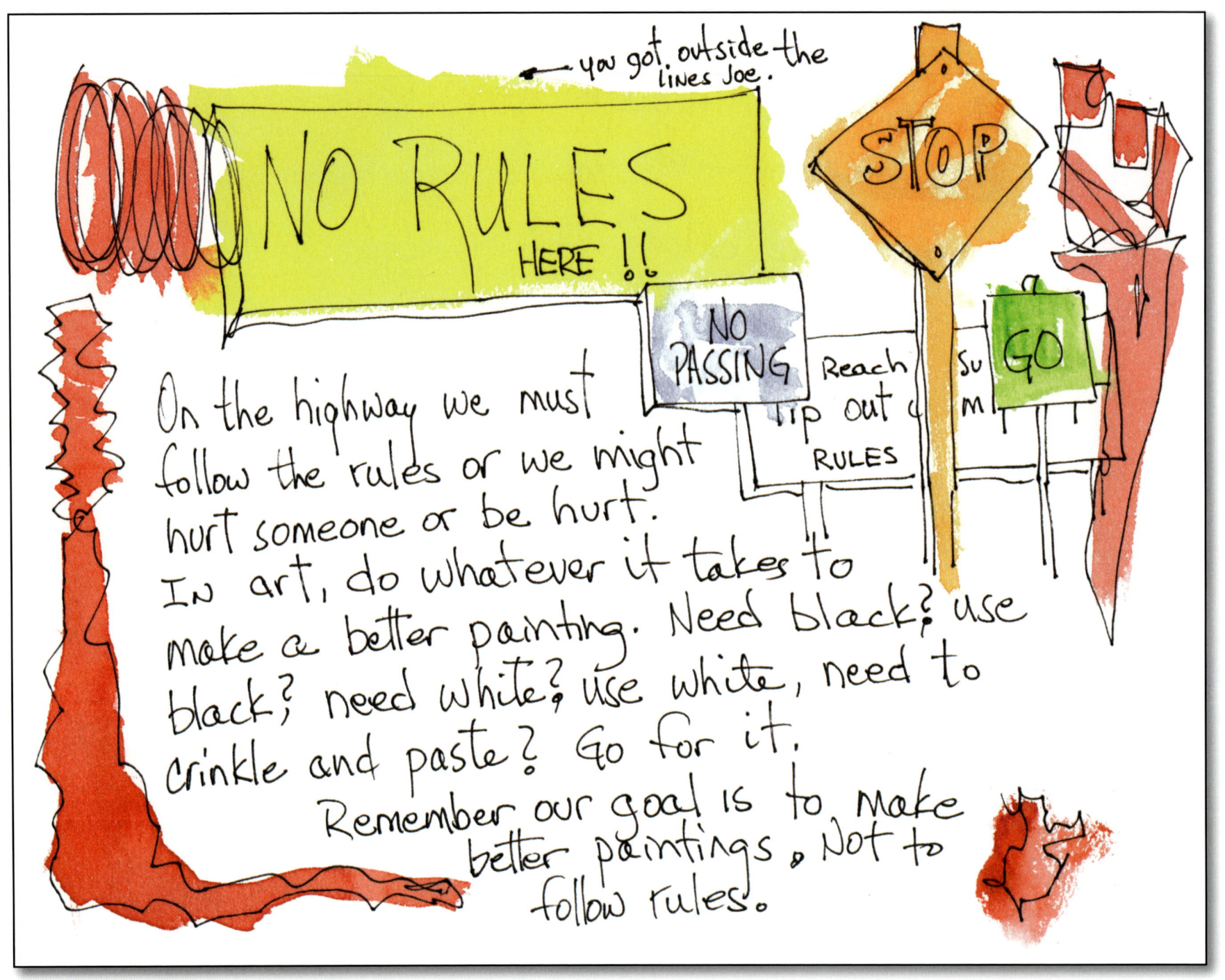

Masking Fluid

Here are several things about masking fluid, which is a rubber-cement type product made especially for watercolor to save white paper.

1. Never, never, never, never put a dry brush in your masking fluid. If you do, it will never, never, never be the same brush again. So, all you have to do is wet your brush thoroughly before dipping it in masking fluid. When finished, simply rinse the brush in water until all the masking fluid is removed.
2. Try using sticks to apply masking fluid. I find twigs from the woods work well, as do skewers, matchsticks, etc.
3. Try applying masking fluid using a stiff string like bailing twine that farmers use to bail hay with. It will keep you loose, and you won't mess up a brush.
4. You can add color to your masking fluid if you have the white kind. Add a little Cobalt Blue or any non-staining color. Then when you apply it to the paper, you will be able to see the masking fluid easier.

Never, ever put a dry brush in masking fluid. Wet your brush thoroughly before putting it in masking fluid.

On Bamboo Road - Watercolor on Cresent board - 22" x 30"

The Cottage of '93 - Watercolor on Yupo - 15" x 20"

Yupo

Yupo paper comes with "automatic texture" — you just can't paint on it without getting texture and usually lots of it. Yupo has become a major surface for many professional artists such as Taylor Ikin, George James, Mary Ann Beckwith, and others.

Yupo can be difficult to handle — generally speaking, you have to use more color and less H2O. The color isn't absorbed by the Yupo, and that means it lifts very easily. Be careful! When finished, you may "fix" it by spraying with a fixative. One of the advantages of Yupo is that it can be framed without glass, making it lightweight and easy to ship and hang.

A New Use For Rubber Bands

If you paint from photos or value studies or pictures of any kind, here's a quick and easy way to grid them, making it easier to transfer to your paper.

1. Photo

2. Photo with 4 rubber bands around it divided into thirds

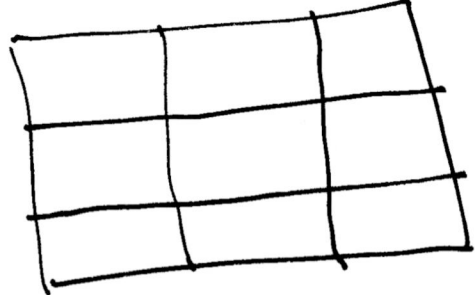

3. Watercolor Paper

4. WC paper with light pencil marks proportional to photo grid.

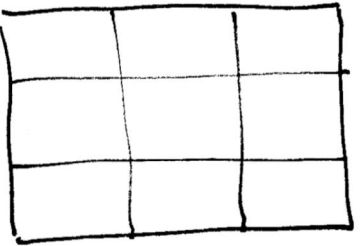

Ready to slop on some paint.

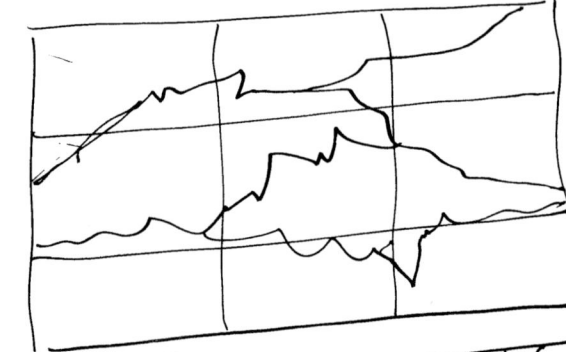

W.C. PAPER

Photo

Some seemingly insignificant little things

Wedging

I like the wedging composition, as it seems to fit our North Carolina mountains.

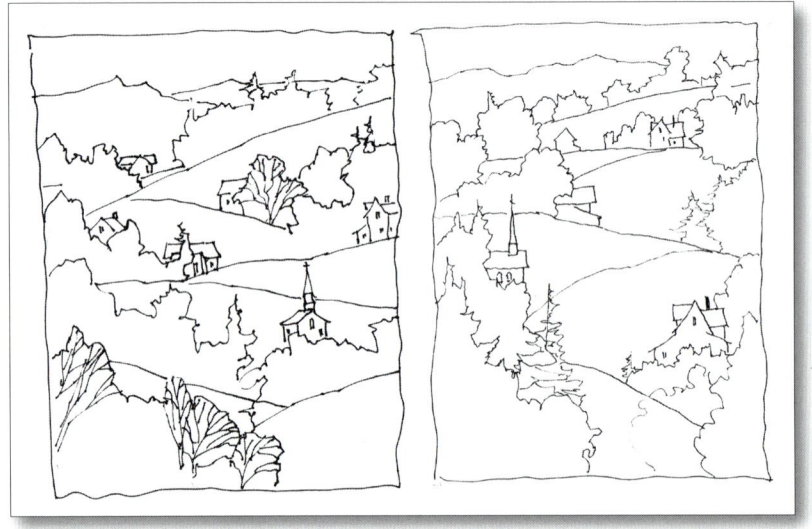

Pen and Ink outline for painting - *Glens of Grandfather*

I think I used a Pitt pen to do these sketches. I really like these pens—they are waterproof and permanent and cheap! And they come in a variety of colors and tip sizes.

Glens of Grandfather - Watercolor on Kilimanjaro 140# cold pressed paper - 20" x 15"

A very early watercolor painted in 1986. I tried to make it appear that there were two paintings lying on a third larger one.

I'm not sure I've made many advances in my art but I can tell you for sure that art has advanced my life tremendously.

Three In One - Watercolor - 20" x 30"

SOME SEEMINGLY INSIGNIFICANT LITTLE THINGS

My Mistakes

Learning to paint, to become an artist is not a linear process. There is not a road map with numbers to teach you. You will and must take the wrong road time and again. I will make it too light and then too dark, too small, too big until one day I get it right, and the light comes on—"I've got it by golly, by jingo!!" On my very next painting I dribble water in the sky and ruin it! Now I know not to let my loaded brush pass over an area I've already painted. I make mistake after mistake, I seem to "get" one thing, only to fail somewhere else. I've learned from my failures, and I find new failures and new lessons all the time. I find that exciting. Learning new things helps keep us young. I just don't want to learn them all in one day!

These little abstract pieces are really fun to do. They were painted over a failed watercolor done on rough 300# paper—so I already had a beginning.

Using acrylics and a piece of mat board for a brush, pick up acrylic on the edge of a little piece of mat board or cardboard, then "pull" that over your watercolor. Repeat this step with a different color until you get the results you like.

Acrylic on 300# rough watercolor paper

I love trying to turn a disaster into something that pleases me. Sometimes I do and sometimes I don't.

Acrylic on 300# rough watercolor paper

SOME SEEMINGLY INSIGNIFICANT LITTLE THINGS

The Well

The journalist Bill Moyers interviewed the mythologist Joseph Campbell and asked him, "If you could say just one thing to young people, what would it be?" Without hesitation Joseph replied, "Follow your bliss." He went on to say, that when you follow your bliss, you will always have it. If you follow money or fame and lose, you've lost it all. When you follow your bliss you may not become wealthy, but you will always have enough and in happiness you will be rich. Another way to say this is, Trust your gut. If you have a gut feeling, you can believe it. If it's just in your head, your brain may try to talk you out of trusting and believing in yourself. Not so with your gut.

If your love, or your bliss, is to make art, then nothing can stop you except yourself, and yourself won't stop you if you won't listen to the negative voice in your head. Will you have times of discouragement or as my sweet little `ole grandmother would say, "get a sinking feeling"? Of course you will. I've been painting for about 25 years now, and I'm sure I had a sinking feeling on

The Well – continued

my first painting, just as I had on the painting I did yesterday! For me now, it's generally the middle of a painting when I think, "This is not working." I keep on slinging paint, and sometimes I end up with a painting I am pleased with. Every creative endeavor has slumps or downturns or sinking feelings. It's part of the creative process. I ran into a artist friend of mine on the sidewalk in front of my drugstore one day and, he asked how my painting was going. "Not so good," I told him. "I seem to be in a slump." he replied, "That's normal." He went on to explain that creative people have to go back to the well. We work and work and we become empty. "Don't fight it—it happens to everyone," he said. This "slump" is simply a time to "refill," to rejuvenate. When it's time to paint again, you will. And you'll probably find you've reached a new, higher level in your work. You'll wonder where it came from. It came from the well.

Chapter 7

Greeting Cards

I enjoy making and sending cards—I enjoy hearing people say, "I loved your card!" Makes me feel good, too.

Some greeting cards I have made

When I give some thought to what I will paint, how, which colors, etc., then make a card, write my message, put my card in the envelope, seal, stamp, and mail it, boy do I get a good feeling. I feel like I really am an artist and I am doing exactly what I'm supposed to be doing. That's part of what it's all about! Making a card for a friend who's been through a tough time always makes me feel better.

Cards I have made

GREETING CARDS

Steps I Follow When I Make a Card.

1. Blank card

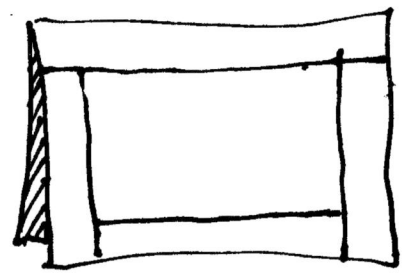

2. Blank card with artist tape around outside border. Be sure to put tape on your shirt or pants before putting it on the card. This will remove some of the tack so it won't tear the card when you remove it.

3. Painting done while tape is still on the card.

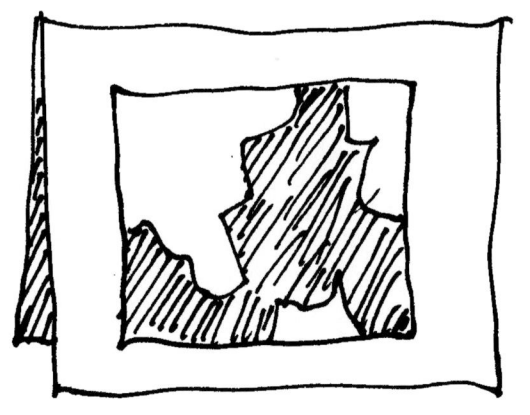

4. Card painted, tape removed

5. Add title or dedication, sign and mail! Satisfaction.

A really easy way to make cards is to take one of your discarded paintings and, by using mats smaller than the original, go over the painting until you find "better paintings" in the larger one. Here is an example using a 4" x 6" white mat, the perfect size for a greeting card. Once I find my card, I draw around the inside of the mat, then cut it out with scissors. Using ATG or double-stick tape, attach it to a blank greeting card, add your message, and send it to a friend!

I start with a painting that I am not to happy with.

GREETING CARDS

Then, with my mats, I begin the search for greeting card pictures within the painting. It is really a lot of fun!

The possibilities are almost endless.

GREETING CARDS

Chapter 8

Other Stuff

Some friends, reflections, laughs, and more...

If you want to do a watercolor, then do a watercolor. Even if you don't know one thing about it. In so doing you will learn. Now do it again. We learn by doing...and doing. And doing.

My Brother
Cheng Khee Chee

Two Trees in a Field of Andrew's Turquoise Painted on Masa paper in a Cheng Khee workshop - 15" x 20"

Painted in a Cheng Khee Chee workshop at Kanuga in Hendersonville, North Carolina. This is just one of Cheng Khee Chee's techniques found in his book <u>The Traditional Watercolor Approach</u>. He usually demos this in his workshops. It's done on wet, crinkled Masa paper using Sumi ink and a couple of colors. To learn more on this technique, refer to his book. Cheng Khee and I became brothers at a workshop in Kanuga, and I have admired and loved him and his wonderful wife, Sing Bee, ever since. We don't see each other very often, but it's one of those friendships that when we come together, no time has passed. I love Cheng Khee and Sing Bee.

To Thine Own Self Be True

Skip Lawrence

I'd walk a mile for a Camel. Remember when this was the Camel cigarette ad? Well, I'd drive 100 miles to study with Skip Lawrence. His was one of the first watercolor workshops I attended. It was in the 1980s while I was still practicing pharmacy but was obsessed with watercolor painting. The workshop was in Greensboro, NC, and I lived in Boone, 100 miles away. Every morning I would leave Boone around 6:30, drive to Greensboro, attend class from 9 to 4, drive back to Boone, and work in the pharmacy till it closed between 10 and 11 p.m. It's a wonder I made it back home safely, because all I could think of was what Skip had taught that day. At that time Skip was doing wonderful, traditional watercolors, all planned with value studies, stretched paper-the whole works. Everybody loved 'em.

Walter Robinson - Collection of Joe Miller - 22" x 30"

Morning Delivery - Collection of Joe Miller - 22" x 30"

Skip's Old-Style Paintings

Then some years later Skip reinvented watercolor. Using almost no water and pure watercolor, he crafted these brilliant, vibrant, eye-catching paintings.

Some people who signed up for his workshops weren't real happy with the change. They wanted the old Skip style. But Skip listened to the voice in his heart. He stayed the course, followed his bliss, and stayed true to his own self.

Desire - Acrylic on canvas - Acrylic on canvas - 40" x 40"

Christmas '09 - Acrylic on canvas - 48" x 48"

Learning - Acrylic on canvas - 60" x 72"

Skip's New Paintings

Before long, other artists not only accepted his new direction but began to imitate it. There's a real lesson for all of us here: **Follow your bliss.**

Skip's work can be seen online at www.skiplawrence.com

OTHER STUFF

Skip 'n Joe - Watercolor - 20' x 30"

I started this painting in a Skip Lawrence workshop. Skip came by and I said, "Tell me what it needs." Instead of telling me, he added the brush vase and brushes. We both signed it, and now I have one of the world's fewest Skip/Joe paintings!

A Life of Sharing
Gerald Brommer

Gerald Brommer has taught so many students for so many years that I can't count that high. Every single person loves and admires him and his lovely wife, Georgia. After a couple of classes with Gerald, I know why we all admire him. He gives and gives and gives.

Street Corner in Colle Val D'Elsa - Watercolor - 22" x 30"

The Gardener's Dream - Watercolor - 15" x 22"

He would be the first to tell you that what he gave to us came back to him tenfold.

My friend Gerald tells about the time he was teaching third grade. "We're going to have a fire drill today, children," he told them. "When the fire bell rings, we will all leave the building, cross the parking lot, and go to the very top of that little hill over there. Does anyone know why we go all the way to the top of that hill?" A little girl who was usually very quiet jumped up and answered, "So we will have a better view of the building burning."

OTHER STUFF

The Rapids at Red Rock on the New River - Collage on canvas - 18" x 18"

A collage done in a Gerald Brommer workshop. I never thought I would be tearing up paper and gluing it to more paper— but I really had fun. And fun is good!

Letters from an Artist Friend
Wayne Atkinson – 7/10/1926 to 9/24/2009

My artist friend Wayne Atkinson mailed me lots of letters, every one in a hand-painted envelope! I've saved every one of them. Real treasures they are. The letters always include a joke or two. I've shown Wayne's envelopes to lots of artists and friends and used his jokes in many of my talks to art groups around the country. What follows are a few of Wayne's envelopes and jokes.

Wayne took his larger paintings, reduced them and printed them on envelopes. He enjoyed doing this and I certainly enjoyed receiving them. Good memories of a good friend.

A man walks into a restaurant and asks, "How do you prepare your chickens?"
The cook says, "Nothing special. We just tell them they're gonna die."

"Madam Fortune Teller, tell me: Are there golf courses in heaven?"
"I have good news and I have bad news."
"What's the good news?"
"The good news is that the golf courses in heaven are beautiful beyond anything you could imagine."
"That's wonderful."
"But, you'll be teeing off at 8:30 tomorrow morning."

My Friend
Janet Walsh

I don't remember when I first met Janet Walsh, but I can tell you I was impressed from day one! I knew I was in the presence of a wonderful artist and shortly knew I was also in the presence of a fine business person. She was both in one.

Some folks are gifted with painting ability....some with business savvy. Usually you'll find your strength in one or the other, but Janet exemplifies both. Not only has Janet earned a respected place in the art world as a painter, but she has used her business skills to further art appreciation. As president of the American Watercolor Society she used her commercial ability to share and further her love of art. Under her guidance, the numbers and the presence of AWS grew to a new level. Her passion for art, combined with her understanding of organization proved to be very effective.

All the while, Janet is your friend. She is a particular friend to me, inviting me into her art world as well as into her personal world. I am a more intuitive painter for having walked paths and shared joys (and sorrows too) with Janet.

OTHER STUFF

Anytime we do an activity
that causes us to lose track of time
and space, it's a good thing.

Except of course,
drinking too much scotch!

A Day in the Life of Cheap Joe's

You've heard the statement "There are no stupid questions." Don't believe it! In the Cheap Joe's store we have had some...."

"How many squirts are in a tube?"

"What colors do I mix to get a sunset?"

"Why don't you have a tube of rainbow color?"

"Do you take cash over the phone?"

A customer called after receiving an order and claimed to have been cheated out of 282 pounds of paper! They said they ordered and paid for 300 pounds of paper and had only got eighteen pounds. After we checked on the order we found: 25 sheets of 300# Arches Cold Pressed—which weighs 18 pounds.

Vincent

Cypress on a Road - after Van Gogh - Acrylic on canvas

Did you know there are three very famous artists known mostly by their first name?

1. Vincent (van Gogh)
2. Leonardo (Da Vinci)
3. Michelangelo (Buonarroti)

I wonder if I will be known by my first name— "Cheap"?

I'm an admirer of Vincent Van Gogh and have used his work to draw inspiration from. If you want to read some of the world's greatest letters, read, <u>Dear Theo</u>, letters written by Vincent to his brother, Theo. If you are the least bit interested in art, you'll really enjoy reading some of Vincent's letters.

It's the Little Things

One of the least understood but greatest needs of all is the need to belong – to be part of something larger than ourselves. Artists do that! We, as artists, belong. Let me tell you just how much my friend Vincent needed to belong. In 1879, Vincent van Gogh attended a school of evangelism, and he graduated from that school. When you finished in that school, they sent you to a place called the Borinage. It was a horrible place in the coal-mining district of Belgium.

They had mined it so much, that dust from the mines had killed all the vegetation. So, it was a very bleak area. It was also in the middle of winter when he went there, with snow on the ground. He had fine clothes, and the miners, of course, had clothing woven from burlap. And they were dirty, because they had very little water and certainly no hot water to wash themselves with. In an effort to belong and be part of these people, Vincent traded all of his good clothes for the burlap clothing. And every morning when he got up, he would rub his hands in the coal bucket full of black dust and then rub them on his face – just to belong. It's a great need to belong, and I think we reach a place in life where we begin to wonder what legacy we will leave behind. Who will remember me and for what? For most of us, it will probably be the little things we did for someone, the smile when someone was down, the pat on the back, an encouraging word – perhaps we helped someone get started in art. It most likely will not be anything monumental, like inventing the light bulb or the wheel or signing a major peace treaty. Perhaps leaving a few pieces of our art for our children or loved ones will be monumental enough.

Lighthouse at Little River, South Carolina - Watercolor - 30" x 22"

There's an old proverb that goes something like this: King Solomon wrote a book of proverbs, but a book of proverbs never made a King Solomon. I watch artists do a demo. I go immediately to my art table to do what I just observed, and unless I took really good notes, I don't even know where to start. Did he draw first or not at all—what was the next thing. I take really good notes and I refer to them and I still can't do what I just saw. Not even close.

Why? Because I haven't experienced it before. I will have to try and try again. I will fail many times before I come close. I don't despair, I don't give up, and with practice I will achieve some success. I can never be another artist. I can only be Joe and I can only have Joe's style. I will follow my heart, paint my own subjects, my life, with my colors and I will be happy with some or all of what I do—life is better this way!

Midnight in Creston, N.C. - Watercolor - 20" x 30" - Private Collection

I used three colors in this night scene: French Ultramarine, Brown Madder, and Raw Sienna. It's a painting I did some years ago, but I still like it. I think all artists think, I could have done better. But one day it dawned on me—if I could have done better, why hadn't I? Because at the time, this was my best effort! I did the best I could do.

Some artists are never satisfied with their work. I'm not one of those. Sometimes I like what I painted a lot, sometimes a little, and yes, sometimes none. I would become discouraged if once in a while I wasn't pleased with my work. When someone says, "I really do like that painting of yours", I say, "Thanks, I do too!" When someone compliments you, believe them.

Seeing for the First Time

Tampa Bay - Watercolor - 12" x 20" - Collection of Mr. & Mrs. Mark Hodges.

I love traveling—seeing new scenes, new shapes. Its inspires me to paint. I've learned that when I see a new scene, it's important that I sketch it then and there. If I don't and I continue to see it, it, the scene becomes common and I never paint it. Sometimes when I travel to a new place it takes me a few days to "settle in." I may be anxious to sketch or paint and I even see scenes that excite me, but it seems as though I need some time to just be—to look, to absorb the colors and the feeling of the place. Then I can sketch and paint.

On #2 at Red Tail Mountain Golf Course, Mt. City, Tennessee - Watercolor - 15" x 30"   Collection of Sam and Jackie Adams

I passed the above scene many times and never really "saw it." Then one day while playing golf with friends, one of my friends said, "Joe, that looks like a place you'd like to paint." Wow! Someone else had to point it out to me. When new artists come to Boone to teach or paint and I have the good fortune of showing them around the area, I'm always surprised by what they see. It's usually a place I've driven by dozens of times and never really seen. To see out of another's eyes is like seeing a place for the first time.

Rooster Crow - Watercolor - 20" x 30"

The idea for this painting came from a fishing trip. I was float fishing the Watauga River in Tennessee for trout early one foggy morning when off in the distance was this scene. I did a quick sketch, made a few notes, and did this painting—mostly wet/wet—when I got home. P.S. Caught lots of fish!

I was born in the mountains of North Carolina, and I will probably die here. I never tire of looking out over the Blue Ridge Mountains. I love painting them too. My good friend Noyes Capehart once told me, "Paint what you know, what you love." I've tried to be true to that.

Roan Valley Community - Watercolor - 15" x 20"

ART: the more you do it, the better you get at it.

South Carolina Marsh - Watercolor - 20" x 30" - Private Collection

Be Grateful for the Small Blessings.

Glen is an old World War II Veteran who never married and by any standards is very poor. His house has gravity-fed water, heat from a wood stove, and few other conveniences. He receives Meals on Wheels and has Medicaid, Medicare and veterans' assistance. He has one sister who lives a great distance away. By now you get the picture. I was sitting on his little front porch in one of those old, green metal lawn chairs visiting with Glen. It was a hot day for Boone, probably 84-85 degrees. I was aware that the floor under my rocker was partially rotten and the white paint was peeling off the side of the house. We were making small talk. A nice gentle breeze shifted across the porch, and Glenn looked at me, smiled, and said, "Boy, what a nice breeze. I always get a good breeze here."

Well, this is the end of this book, but it's not the end of anything else. I hope that today is the beginning of something new and exciting for you whether you are a stark beginner or a professional artist. Remember, old creative people never retire—why would they? Picasso, Michelangelo, Milford Zornes, Monet, Andrew Wyeth, etc. all did art till the very end. That's my plan too!

Sincerely,

Your Friend always,